THE NAMES

Also by
N. Scott Momaday

HOUSE MADE OF DAWN
THE WAY TO RAINY MOUNTAIN
ANGLE OF GEESE AND OTHER POEMS
THE GOURD DANCER

New York, Hagerstown, San Francisco, London

THE NAMES

A Memoir by
N. SCOTT MOMADAY

HARPER & ROW, PUBLISHERS

FIRST EDITION

Designed by Gloria Adelson
Photo reproductions by Jim Kalett

Library of Congress Cataloging in Publication Data

Momaday, N   Scott, 1934–
    The names.

    1. Momaday, N. Scott, 1934–   —Biography—
Youth. 2. Authors, American—20th century—
Biography. I. Title.
PS3563.047Z52   813'.5'4 [B]   75-138749
ISBN 0–06–012981–6

76 77 78 79 80 10 9 8 7 6 5 4 3 2 1

In devotion

to those whose names I bear

and to those who bear my names

Genealogical chart

Kaw-au-ointy m. Ah-kgoo-ahu

I. J. Galyen m. Natachee

Pohd-lohk

Keahdinekeah m. Guipagho

Nancy m. George Scott

Mammedaty m. Aho

Theodore m. Anne Ellis

Huan-toa (Alfred)
m. Natachee

Tsoai-talee (NSM)

My name is Tsoai-talee. I am, therefore, Tsoai-talee; therefore I am.

The storyteller Pohd-lohk gave me the name Tsoai-talee. He believed that a man's life proceeds from his name, in the way that a river proceeds from its source.

In general my narrative is an autobiographical account. Specifically it is an act of the imagination. When I turn my mind to my early life, it is the imaginative part of it that comes first and irresistibly into reach, and of that part I take hold. This is one way to tell a story. In this instance it is my way, and it is the way of my people. When Pohd-lohk told a story he began by being quiet. Then he said Ah-keah-de, "They were camping," and he said it every time. I have tried to write in the same way, in the same spirit. Imagine: They were camping.

PROLOGUE

You know, everything had to begin, and this is how it was: the Kiowas came one by one into the world through a hollow log. They were many more than now, but not all of them got out. There was a woman whose body was swollen up with child, and she got stuck in the log. After that, no one could get through, and that is why the Kiowas are a small tribe in number. They looked all around and saw the world. It made them glad to see so many things. They called themselves **Kwuda,** *"coming out."*

Kiowa folk tale

They were stricken, surely, nearly blind in the keep of some primordial darkness. And yet it was their time, and they came out into the light, one after another, until the way out was lost to them. Loss was in the order of things, then, from the beginning. Their emergence was a small thing in itself, and unfinished. But it gave them to know that they were and who they were. They could at last say to themselves, "We are, and our name is *Kwuda*."

Pohd-lohk. They say he made fine arrows.

ONE

THE NAMES AT FIRST are those of animals and of birds, of objects that have one definition in the eye, another in the hand, of forms and features on the rim of the world, or of sounds that carry on the bright wind and in the void. They are old and original in the mind, like the beat of rain on the river, and intrinsic in the native tongue, failing even as those who bear them turn once in the memory, go on, and are gone forever: Pohd-lohk, Keahdinekeah, Aho.*

And Galyen, Scott, McMillan, whose wayfaring lay in the shallow traces from Virginia and Louisiana, who knew of blooded horses and tobacco and corn whiskey, who preserved in their songs the dim dialects of the Old World.

The land settles into the end of summer. In the white light a

*A glossary of Indian terms will be found on page 168.

whirlwind moves far out in the plain, and afterwards there is something like a shadow on the grass, a tremor, nothing. There seems a stillness at noon, but that is illusion: the landscape rises and falls, ringing. In the dense growth of the bottomland a dark drift moves on the Washita River. A spider enters a small pool of light on Rainy Mountain Creek, and downstream, at the convergence, a Channel catfish turns around in the current and slithers to the surface, where a dragonfly hovers and darts. Away on the high ground grasshoppers and bees set up a crackle and roar in the fields, and meadowlarks and scissortails whistle and wheel about. Somewhere in a maze of gullies a calf shivers and bawls in a tangle of chinaberry trees. And high in the distance a hawk turns in the sun and sails.

Gyet'aigua. Where you been?
'Cross the creek.
'S'hot, ain'it?

The angle of the Washita River and Rainy Mountain Creek points to the east, and the thick red waters descend into the depths of the Southern Plains, as if they measure by means of an old, organic equation the long way from the Continental Divide to the heart of North America. This angle is a certain delineation on the face of the Great Plains, an idea of geometry in the mind of God.

The light there is of a certain kind. In the mornings and evenings it is soft and pervasive, and the earth seems to absorb it, to become enlarged with light. About the noons there are edges and angles—and a brightness that is hard and thin like a glaze. There is something strange and powerful in it. When you look out across the land you believe at first that it is all one thing; there appears to be an awful sameness to it. But after a while you see that it is not one thing at all, but many things, all of which are subject to change in a moment. At times the air is thick and languid, and you imagine that the world

4

has grown very old and tired. At other times the air is full of motion and commotion. Always a hard weather impends upon the plains. In advance of a storm the plains are a strange and beautiful thing to see, concentrated in random details, distances; there are slow, massive movements.

> There in the hollow of the hills I see,
> Eleven magpies stand away from me.
>
> Low light upon the rim; a wind informs
> This distance with a gathering of storms
>
> And drifts in silver crescents on the grass,
> Configurations that appear, and pass.
>
> There falls a final shadow on the glare,
> A stillness on the dark, erratic air.
>
> I do not hear the longer wind that lows
> Among the magpies. Silences disclose,
>
> Until no rhythms of unrest remain,
> Eleven magpies standing in the plain.
>
> They are illusion—wind and rain revolve—
> And they recede in darkness, and dissolve.

Water runs in planes on the earth, in ropes in the cuts of the banks; the wind lunges; lightning is constant on the cold, black hemisphere; and everything is visible, strangely visible. Oh Man-ka-ih!

Some of my earliest memories are of the storms, the hot rain lashing down and lightning running on the sky—and the storm cellar into which my mother and I descended so many times when I was very young. For me that little room in the earth is an unforgettable place. Across the years I see my mother reading there on the low, narrow bench, the lamplight flickering on her face and on the earthen walls; I smell the dank odor of that room; and I hear the great weather raging at the door. I have never been in a place that was like it exactly; only now and then I have been reminded of it suddenly when I have gone into a cave, or when I have just caught the scent of fresh, open earth steaming in the rain, and I have been for a moment startled and strangely glad in the presence of the past, the mother and child. But at times as I look back I see the fear in my mother's face, a hard vigilance in the attitude of her whole body, for hail is beating down upon the door, and the roar of the wind is deafening; the earth and sky are at odds, and God shudders. Even now, after many years of living in another landscape, my mother will not go into that wide corridor of the Great Plains but that she does so with many misgivings and keeps a sharp eye on the sky.

> The terrapins crawl up on the hills.
> They know, ain'it? The terrapins know.
> A day, two days before, they go.

2

Or I am in the arbor. It is an August day in 1934. My mother and father watch over me, swing me in a little hammock, hum to me a lullaby. My grandmother Aho is there, too, and my uncles James, Lester, Ralph. I have no notion of time; the moment does not exist for me as time, but it exists only as pain or puzzlement, perhaps a sound, a word. What I shall come to know as time is now an imperceptible succession of colors, of dawns and dusks, mornings and afternoons, a concentration of days into one day, or it is simply the inside of eternity, the hollow of a great wing. These are the things I know: the slow, summer motion of the air, the shadows that gather upon the walls, birds crisscrossing at the screen, the rhythms within

The arbor. It is a place of strong magic. My father was born on this site. Here Pohd-Lohk gave me my Indian name.

me. And I know the voices of my parents, of my grandmother, of others. Their voices, their words, English and Kiowa—and the silences that lie about them—are already the element of my mind's life.

Zei-dl-bei. Brush the flies away.

Had I known it, even then language bore all the names of my being.

Water is drawn from the well, the sound of the pulley creaking, the bucket scraping upon the long metal sleeve in the shaft, the bucket scraping upon the ear.

Raff, you got any hooks? Let's set out some lines tonight. Half moon. There's rain in the north.
Yeah, okay.
Where's the lantern, the good one?
Shoot, you had it. It's in the cellar, I guess. You had it last time.

My father's people are arrogant and set in their ways. I like this in them, for it gives them a certain strength of character, a color and definition of their own. But it means that they are hard to suffer, too. This distemper of theirs was a very serious matter to my mother about the time of her marriage. She came warily among the Kiowas. That is a whole story, hers to tell; yet some part of it is mine as well. And there is a larger story; I think of where I am in it.

3

About the year 1850 in Kentucky a daughter was born to I. J. Galyen and his Cherokee wife, Natachee, newcomers to the knobs from the foothills of the Great Smoky Mountains. Very little is known of I. J. Galyen, and even less is known of his bride. Perhaps there was Indian blood in his veins, too; family tradition has it that he was predominantly French (Gallien?). He settled in the countryside known as "the knobs," for its numerous abrupt hills, in southwestern Kentucky. Natachee bore him four children, one of whom was Nancy Elizabeth, my great-grandmother. Nancy was frail, sallow-skinned, altogether quiet. She married George Scott of Woodbury and bore him five children. Her first son was Theodore, my grandfather.

My mother tells me that the ancestral house at Scott's Landing was built in 1784. Charles Scott was a general in the Revolutionary War and the fourth governor of Kentucky (1808–1812); he commanded Kentucky troops in the War of 1812.

There is a roiling rain, so fine that it remains in the air like a scent. There are barns in the trees, smoking. Smoke, a little darker, denser than the sky, rises from the cracks in the walls and hangs above the woods. The broad sidings are gray and black slats, rough-surfaced, frosted with age like old men. In the dark doors the big brown and yellow sheaves hang heavy and still, shriveled, yet swollen with smoke and damp.

I have been to the graves of two of my great-great-grandparents, one on each side of my family. I. J. Galyen and his daughter Nancy are buried close together on the edge of a thick, tangled woods. There are trees in Smith Cemetery, but they are apart from the woods, which are wild. Trees that stand among tombstones are singular and discrete in their definition; their roots extend into the strict society of the dead.

My mother and I once stood at the foot of Nancy Scott's grave. A man approached through the fields, a long way, and greeted us. He was large, rude in appearance; a shotgun lay in the crook of his neck.

George Scott and his family. Theodore, my grandfather, sits on his mother's lap.

He was dressed in a plaid shirt and overalls, high, heavy shoes, and a rumpled brown felt hat. His face was almost perfectly round, and his teeth were remarkably small and brown-stained. He did not smile, but he was amiable. I thought: This man must know odd and interesting things, and he must know them well.

Reckon it's gon' rine. M'nime's Belcher. Y'all got folk hyere? They's wald chickens in them woods.
Y'all listen; you c'n hyear them wald chickens by.
It's gon' rine.

Theodore Scott was born in 1875. He was a third child and first son. Before him were born Olivia and Myrtle; after him Granville and Elizabeth. When the children were very young their father worked on the railroad, and the family lived at Henderson, on the Ohio River. There George Scott died about 1885 of tuberculosis. Nancy returned with her children to her father's house (I. J. Galyen died in 1878) at Costellow, above Chandler's Chapel.

Tuberculosis ravaged Nancy's family. Her mother the old Cherokee woman is thought to have died of it (but when? and where is she buried?); it is likely that her father was infected; her husband and all three of her daughters were destroyed by it. Only her sons, Theodore and Granville, were spared. They lived to be old men.

Theodore Scott was fourteen when his mother died. Life must have been very hard for him at the time. His elder sisters were already married and had homes and families of their own. He was at an awkward age, neither a man nor a child, and he had to make his way. Soon he was working twelve hours a day for his keep at the farm of a neighbor, Bob Patterson. Once in the middle of the night he was found standing beside his bed, going wearily through the motions of pitching hay in his sleep. He visited his aunt Talitha (Nancy's sister)

11

I. J. Galyen, my great-great-grandfather.

The graves of I. J. Galyen and his daughter Nancy Scott. There are wild chickens in the woods.

I like to think that Theodore looks like his grandmother Natachee here. There is no photograph of her.

on occasion, and there, he remembered years later, was an old woman —his Cherokee grandmother, probably. She gave money to Talitha's children, bright silver coins, but she gave none to him. He did not mind; resentment and self-pity had no part in the remembrance, but it seems a curious thing to me. Perhaps he was thought by the old woman to be too old for such considerations at fifteen.

He kept an eye on his brother, Granville, who more even than the baby, Elizabeth, bore watching. Gran was wild in his spirit and was said to take after his uncles James and Matthew, in whom the Cherokee strain was pronounced, as it was not in Nancy; it seems that Natachee's sons had no use for the ways of civilization and kept to the woods all their lives, hunting, trapping, and fishing. But Gran preferred to express his spirit early and often in terms of outlawry.

> *In Cumberland City I married me a wife,*
> *I loved her as I love my life;*

14

She treated me kind the night and day
And led me to rob on the broad highway.

Once, they say, he pulled a gun on a preacher.

Mornin', Reverend Barlow. Oh me oh my, I surely do admire that
mare of yours, Reverend.
Yes, thank you kindly, and good morning to you, Granville Scott.
I would trade you horses, Reverend.
Yes?
I *will* trade you horses, by God.

Theodore had soon to spend much of the time getting Granville
out of trouble. That is not to say that Theodore was himself always
on the side of the law—there are stories—but his was decidedly the
cooler head, and he had the man of the family's responsibility of
setting a good example.

Theodore Scott was a man of unusual composure. Even in his later
years he was physically straight and compact, anomalously free and
deliberate in his motions. His grip was very strong, stronger I believe
than I, or anyone else, ever knew. But he was *supposed* to be strong,
physically and otherwise. He was a man in whom the sheer strength
of reserve was a principal part. He had blue eyes and dark hair, high
cheekbones, and a high, broad forehead. His expression was pleasant,
as a rule, and he was soft-spoken. He laughed readily, for he found
humor in much of what he saw and heard, in much of what he did
and cared to do. He was a man of steady good will.

The brothers Scott gained a certain reputation as hard young men
of the territory, figures to be acknowledged, reckoned with. For ten
years or more they lived an easy, aimless life in the knob country. But

15

Robie Ellis. He was a Union Soldier.

Granville Scott at Fort Sam Houston.

there was one notable break in the continuum. About 1894 Theodore and Granville Scott went west, presumably on the advice of a doctor who knew of the incidence of tuberculosis in their family history, to Colorado. For two years they worked on the irrigation canals at La Mar and La Junta, riding patrol. Colorado was a wide-open world then. In the brothers this sojourn worked a wonderful contemplation of the American West, a full-blown and lifelong imagining. When they returned to Kentucky they had seen something of the great world, particularly that legendary part of it which in the last decade of the nineteenth century was still a frontier. They returned to Kentucky, then, the "dark and bloody hunting ground" of an earlier frontier, with a new and larger sense of the continent. They would never again see the green, wooded landscape of the knobs in the same way, and they would both come to the end of their lives far west of the Mississippi.

In time they went off again, to join the army; and they were billeted at Fort Sam Houston, Texas. There is a photograph of Theodore Scott in soldier blue, strumming a banjo.

> *The shanghai ran off and the cattle all died,*
> *The last piece of bacon that morning was fried;*
> *Poor Ike got discouraged, and Betsy got mad,*
> *The dog wagged his tail and looked wonderful sad.*

And at last they went their separate ways. Theodore in 1901 married a woman who was five years older than he. Anne Elizabeth Ellis was handsome and good-hearted, with dark hair and blue eyes. She had been married (to Virgil Bellow?) and borne a child, a daughter who died in infancy. Her marriage had died with the child; she waited. Her father was Robie Ellis of Chandler's Chapel. His given name was that of a Creole forebear, and his people had come from Louisiana. Her mother was a McMillan.

18

Grandmother. The Red black in its channel; mosses black at the long bark; an orange moon; moonlit sloughs.

Anne Elizabeth was quiet, affectionate, generous. These were qualities that Theodore Scott understood well and required absolutely. He placed a simple gold band on her finger and set about the making of a married man's life. From Bob Patterson he had learned how to grow tobacco, how to tell the intrinsic character of the leaf in its veins, precisely how to cut and cure the hands. Tobacco was to be close to his heart throughout his life, as it is close to the hearts of many Kentuckians, who understand in their blood that its value consists not only in the cash for which it is given in trade, but also in the remembered wilderness that was given up for it, the hundreds of thousands of acres of cherry, walnut, and maple trees that were cleared to make a plant bed. Tobacco—the fields, the barns, the busy floors—became a natural and singular expression of the region, like the bluegrass and the limestone. But the knobs were not suited to the growing of tobacco, and Theodore fetched his bride down to the broad plain of the Little River in Christian County, close to the floors at Hopkinsville. He settled at Fairview, a hamlet on the Todd County line, notable as the birthplace of Jefferson Davis, president of the Confederate States of America.

Robie Ellis had been a Union soldier, unaccountably. He was a narrow, hard-edged man; and he said of Anne Elizabeth's children, his grandchildren: They will all be hanged by the time they are twenty for their damned Indian blood.

Fairview was otherwise a place of strong Southern sentiment.

> *I can't take up my musket*
> *And fight 'em now no mo';*
> *But I ain't a-goin' to love 'em,*

19

Now that is sartin sho;
And I don't want no pardon
For what I was and am,
And I won't be reconstructed,
AND I DON'T GIVE A DAMN.

Three children were born to Anne Elizabeth and Theodore Scott: Ethel in 1904, Leslie (a boy) in 1906, and Mayme Natachee, my mother, in 1913. Theodore worked hard but did not prosper, and he was restless. With the advent of World War I he removed his family to Edwardsville, Illinois (Granville had preceded him there), where he found work in a tool factory. At Edwardsville, in the great influenza epidemic of 1918, a plague which spread to forty-six states and killed nearly half a million people, Anne Elizabeth died in her forty-eighth year. Theodore returned with his children to Kentucky. He did not cherish and sustain his grief, as some men do; nor did he marry again.

My mother is the namesake of that dark mystery, the wife of I. J. Galyen. Kentucky determined her. Once she discoursed to me: "Kentucky is justly famous for three things in particular, her women, her horses, and her tobacco." I reminded her of Kentucky bourbon (she was sipping a mint julep at the time), but she dismissed this as an impertinence. We were standing at the rail on the first turn at Churchill Downs, about to see a horse named Proud Clarion, a 30-to-1 shot, upset the field. In 1913, the year my mother was born, a 91-to-1 long shot, Donerail, on a fast track, won the thirty-ninth Kentucky Derby and paid $184.90 on a two-dollar ticket to win. The jockey was a man named Goose.

The baby Natachee was her father's darling; she had her way. She instructed herself to be persecuted, to dissolve into tears, to be poised prettily in the press of some precocious agony. She acquired the disposition of a martyr, and she imagined herself audaciously. When

20

My mother. (Perhaps the doll's name was Natachee, too.)

she was three or four years old she played in the woods where, three generations before, her great-grandmother's people had passed on the Trail of Tears.

Some of my mother's memories have become my own. This is the real burden of the blood; this is immortality. I remember: My mother was very young, four or five years old. Something had gone wrong. My grandfather was away at work. When he came home my mother ran into his arms, sobbing. He was weary, but he took her up and carried her out into the warm evening, drove her along a moonlit road in his surrey. The road runs north from Fairview center through fields and woods beyond, by the cemetery where Robie Ellis is buried and nothing now marks his grave. The surrey creaks and shifts, as if the wheels are walking. The horse plods along, its head hanging. The moonlight works a strange effect upon the fields, a dull radiance that closes all the distances to the circumference of the night. The black woods stand almost far away, flowing very slowly, smoothly against the motion of the surrey. Fireflies signal here and there. The sky is of a color neither blue nor black, and there is nothing in it to be acknowledged beyond the occasional flicker of a star. Only just now a longing like love bears upon the vast, clear indifference of this night.

Ethel and Leslie (called Buddy) left home. Natachee remained with her father. For a time Theodore was a sheriff at Trenton, in the south of Todd County. It was a dangerous job; he shot at people, and people shot at him. It delighted me that, when I came to know him, he slept with a pistol under his pillow.

My mother, the sheriff's daughter, got possession of a handgun. She wanted practice, and she went out of the town to find a target. She found a barn that would do, and she shot the broad side of it full of holes. Only afterwards did she learn that it was the mayor's barn and that one of his blooded mares was inside. She did not shoot the mare;

My mother. There is something Russian or Asian about her here. She has become a beautiful woman.

neither, she said, did she aim to shoot it.

Naturally they were very close, father and daughter. Natachee's devotion was fierce. Theodore was an extremely gentle man, always at peace with himself. I never saw him lose his temper.

The Jefferson Davis Monument at Fairview was dedicated in 1929, one hundred and twenty-one years after Davis' birth. It is an impressive structure, a concrete obelisk which rises 351 feet above a twenty-acre park. It is a principal thing in the landscape. The construction was long and erratic. Natachee and this monument grew up together. In 1929 my mother was a Southern belle; she was about to embark upon an extraordinary life. It was about this time that she

My mother called herself "Little Moon".

began to see herself as an Indian. That dim native heritage became a fascination and a cause for her, inasmuch, perhaps, as it enabled her to assume an attitude of defiance, an attitude which she assumed with particular style and satisfaction; it became her. She imagined who she was. This act of the imagination was, I believe, among the most important events of my mother's early life, as later the same essential act was to be among the most important of my own.

She was already a raving beauty. She had very black hair and very blue eyes; her skin was clear and taut, of an olive complexion, and her bones were fine and well shaped. She moved gracefully and directly, with certain confidence. Above all, she expected the world to be interesting; she would not stand to be bored. Her cousins, who were plain, called her the Queen of Sheba, which pleased her mightily. But she was more particularly Natachee, or "Little Moon," as she sometimes said, and she drew a blanket about her and placed a feather in her hair. And she went off to Haskell Institute, the Indian school at Lawrence, Kansas. Her roommate there was a Kiowa girl, Lela Ware. Destinies began to converge then, in 1929.

That was the year in which the old woman Kau-au-ointy died on the north side of Rainy Mountain Creek and was buried at Rainy Mountain Cemetery, Kiowa County, Oklahoma. Kau-au-ointy had been a captive and a slave. The Kiowas, who stole people as well as horses in their heyday, took her from her homeland of Mexico when she was a child. As it happened with so many of the captives, Kau-au-ointy outlived her slave status, married, and brought new blood to the tribe in her children. The captives represent a strain which was peculiarly the vigor of the Plains culture from the time of contact, I believe. This old slave woman my great-great-grandmother and I were born one hundred years apart. In my dreams she has told me wonderful stories.

25

Sampt'e drew the string back and back until he felt the bow wobble in his hand, and he let the arrow go. It shot across the long light of the morning and struck the black face of a stone in the meadow; it glanced then away towards the west, limping along in the air; and then it settled down in the grass and lay still. Sampt'e approached; he looked at it with wonder and was wary; honestly he believed that the arrow might take flight again, so much of his life did he give into it.

Here, grandma, I brought you some candy—hard, red candy.
Eh neh neh neh neh!

4

Mammedaty was my grandfather, whom I never knew. Yet he came to be imagined posthumously in the going on of the blood, having invested the shadow of his presence in an object or a word, in his name above all. He enters into my dreams; he persists in his name.

Mammedaty was the son of Guipagho the Younger and of Keahdinekeah, one of the wives of Pohd-lohk. His grandfather Guipagho the Elder was a famous chief, for whom the town of Lone Wolf, Oklahoma, is named, and like his father, Mammedaty lived in the reflected glory of a large reputation. All in all, he bore up under that burden, they say, with courage and good will. His mother, Keahdinekeah, was the daughter of Kau-au-ointy, a woman of strong, foreign character. There was a considerable vitality in him, therefore, and a self-respect that verged upon arrogance. He was born in 1880.

Just before Mammedaty's time the Kiowas had been brought to their knees in the infamous winter campaigns of the Seventh Cavalry,

26

Rainy Mountain. Many of my relatives lie
in the cemetery nearby. The grasshoppers
are innumerable.

and their Plains culture, which was relatively new to them, virtually destroyed. Nomads, they had come upon the Southern Plains at about the time of the Revolutionary War, having migrated from the area of the headwaters of the Yellowstone River, in what is now western Montana, by way of the Black Hills and the High Plains. Along the way they had become a people of the deep interior, the midcontinent —hunters, warriors, keepers of the sacred earth. When at long last they drew within sight of the Wichita Mountains, they had conceived a new notion of themselves and of their destiny.

There are many levels to the land, and many colors. You are drawn into it, down and away. You see the skyline, and you are there at once in your mind, and you have never been there before. There is no confinement, only wonder and beauty.

The Kiowas could not remember a time of glory in their racial life; they knew only that they were the "coming out" people, according to the name which they gave to themselves, *Kwuda,* who in their origin myth had entered the world through a hollow log. Now it must have seemed to them that in the Southern Plains of 1800, they had reached the time and place of their fulfillment; and so it was indeed. In the course of their long journey they had acquired horses, the sun dance religion, and a certain love and possession of the prairies. They had become centaurs in their spirit. For a hundred years, more or less, they ruled an area that extended from the Arkansas River to the Staked Plains, from the rain shadow of the Rocky Mountains to the Gulf of Mexico, and in them was realized the culmination of a culture that was peculiarly vital, native, and distinct, however vulnerable and ill-fated. But by the time Mammedaty was born the Kiowas had been routed in the Indian wars, the great herds of buffalo had been destroyed, and the sun dance prohibited by law.

28

Nonetheless Mammedaty had his own life to live, and he thought of being a farmer. The thought must have galled him at first, for the Kiowas were hunters and had never had an agrarian tradition, and indeed they were at best disdainful of their neighbors the Wichitas, Creeks, and Osages, who were planters. And yet he had to contend with the matter of his own survival—a practical matter first, then a spiritual one—and with the example of his closer forebears as well. His grandmother Kau-au-ointy was headstrong and indomitable still, in her sixties, careless of all custom and tradition, and his mother, Keahdinekeah, before she was married, had run her own herd of cattle, riding harder and better than the men who watched her, with grudging admiration, out of the corners of their eyes. And on the other side, too, there was likewise precedent, enough to bridle a young man. Guipagho the Elder was known to make the best of a bad situation, having counseled his people in defeat, urging them simply to hold together when dissolution and degeneration threatened to destroy them. If it came to that, Mammedaty could swallow his pride and be proud of it. Moreover, he had very little choice in the matter. Under the allotment system he had too little land to raise cattle as a business, and the whites had long since begun to close in on all sides, building roads and fences, churches and towns. While many of his kinsmen gave themselves up to self-pity and despair, Mammedaty sowed cotton and wheat, melons and beans.

Shortly after the turn of the century Mammedaty married Aho, the daughter of Gaa-kodalte. She had been a schoolgirl at Rainy Mountain, and somewhere there was in her breeding—as there was in his own—a sheer and separate vitality. It was said that one of her grandfathers was a French Canadian who had come to trade for horses on the Brazos in the 1830s. But for all that she was a Kiowa, sure enough, and a black-eyed beauty besides. And for Mammedaty that was that. In the space of twenty years she bore him six children, two daughters and four sons. Her spirit was whole and hard to bend,

Two kiowa captives sitting in chairs on the prairie. The woman is Kau-au-ointy, my great-great-grandmother.

Aho, my grandmother.

and she should certainly have dominated a weaker character—she found in her eldest son a temperament that she could own and manage precisely—but Mammedaty was his own man. He knew of the gentleness in her and brought it out, as he brought a harvest from the seed. Perhaps he saw at once that beneath the hard surface of her will there was a reserve and thoughtfulness that should—and did in fact—succeed and commemorate him, that she should keep possession of his name in all her ways.

The dark came first into the house. It was so gradual, then there was nothing to see except the windows, the dusk on the grass, the arbor like a great skeleton. Someone touched a match to the wick and fitted the globe down and yellow light grew up in the room. The shadows were thrown up high on the walls; the oilcloth on the oval table gleamed; the flame was like a great yellow tooth.

Mammedaty was shrewd in matters of the world; he spent little and traded well, and so he prospered. There were times when he was out of sorts, and his temper got the better of him on occasion, but in the main he was steady enough. He worked hard and believed in his work, and yet there were more important things in his life. It was in his nature to be religious, and he looked deeply into the spiritual part of things. For a time he wore a medicine bundle around his neck, and he prayed to the sun. At odd moments he beheld strange things, visions to which he attached great, supernatural significance. He was a peyote priest in his prime and a Christian in his last years. His character was such that it could not have been easy for him to give up the one way for the other; he must have been for a long time on the edge of eternity.

How was it then?
We used to go to Cache, to Quanah Parker's house. There were

peyote meetings there. Quanah Parker had a beautiful house; there was a big white star on the roof.

Mammedaty built a house for his mother on the north side of Rainy Mountain Creek, and when he died Keahdinekeah buried him in a bronze casket and covered it with her favorite shawl, and then she lived out her life there in a room of that house, a room that was at last like the shadow in her sightless eyes. And there she dreamed of him, of winter mornings and autumn afternoons in which he was a child, and of the child's delights: new moons and rainbows and wheeling birds.

On a high knoll across the creek Mammedaty built a house for himself and his wife and children. This was 1913, the year in which my father, while the house was under construction, was born in a tipi on the north side of the site, where later the arbor was to be. The youngest of Mammedaty's children, Ralph, was born in the house in 1920, and all but one, a daughter who died in infancy, grew up in it.

Mammedaty went on with his farming as long as he lived, and one by one he put his sons to work in the fields, but it came to nothing in the end. When he died the fields were left fallow, or else they were given under lease to the white farmers of the neighborhood, and so it was from then on.

John, how much do you want for that hog?
Twenty-five dollars.
It ain't worth that, John. It ain't worth more than seventeen, eighteen dollars; I'll give you twenty.
It is worth twenty-five dollars.
How much for that hog, your bottom price?
Twenty-five dollars.
Like hell.

Mammedaty died of Bright's disease in 1932.

Well, have you thought it over, John? *Now* how much do you want
for that there hog?
I have thought it over.
Yes?
I want what I wanted yesterday, twenty-five dollars.
All right. All right.
All right.

5

My father, whose Indian name is Huan-toa, was christened Alfred
Morris; thus did my grandparents do honor to the Alfred Morris who
was a white man and merchant of Mountain View, Oklahoma, in
1913 and a "good man" and friend to the family.

Alfred Morris Mammedaty (the institution of the surname was
adopted by the Kiowas during my grandfather's lifetime) grew up in
the house and arbor, and in the town of Mountain View, across the
creek. He worked in his father's fields and he went to school. He
listened to the word of God at the Rainy Mountain Baptist Church,
and he went with his grandmother Keahdinekeah to pray before the
tal-yi-da-i, the medicine bundles that had been handed down from the
time of the sun dance. He went with Mammedaty in a buckboard to
buy goods at Boke's store at Rainy Mountain, and when his parents
went to Chickasha on the Rock Island Railroad he went with his
brothers to wait for them near the trestle on the Washita River;
Mammedaty, in his stiff white collar, and Aho, in her fringed shawl,
their faces beaming in their frames of braids, threw down jellybeans
and Cracker Jack from the windows of the train.

34

Boke's store at Rainy Mountain. There was
a wonderful commerce here. My father
remembers the cracker barrels.

There came about a great restlessness in my father, I don't know when. I believe that this restlessness is something in the blood. The old free life of the Kiowas on the plains, the deep impulse to run and rove upon the wild earth, cannot be given up easily; perhaps it cannot be given up at all. I have seen in the old men of the tribe, especially, a look of longing and—what is it?—dread. And if dread is the right word, it is a grave thing, graver than the fear of death; it is perhaps the dread of being, of having been in some dark predestination, held still, and in that profoundly shamed.

The corral, the high stone wall: it is a great ring, a well. At night it is perhaps beautiful when the moon shines down upon the many facets and smooths them out, so that the figure is whole and softly defined and gleaming. And inside the ring is nothing, blackness.

By the time he was a young man my father had got enough of farming. He wanted to be an artist, a painter. At Bacone College, where he was a student for a time, he became acquainted with the Creek artist Acee Blue Eagle. When Blue Eagle painted Kiowa war dance figures, my father was his authority on the rich, intricate costumes, so that the work might be as authentic as possible in its detail. For his part my father learned from this collaboration how to mix watercolors, how to apply them delicately, effectively to paper. He became a patient, confident craftsman. And he had otherwise become a tall, good-looking, reckless man. I would grow up learning of his magnetism; he was born with a large talent for being liked and admired, and he must have been fully aware of it by this time. He would attract all kinds of people to him, and he would tend to like them in proportion as they liked him. His real friends would often be lost in a large, promiscuous crowd, and he would not then know who they were.

At some point he moved out of that old world of the Kiowas. Like

My father as a Kiowa swain of the Twenties.

Mammedaty, he would make a life for himself. I know now that this was an act, not of renunciation, but of profound affirmation, and that it required considerable courage and strength. My father was born in a tipi in a world from which it was both necessary and costly to succeed.

6

Natachee Scott left Haskell. She did not want to give her time to school; she wanted to be a writer, a journalist. She was a roving and unpublished correspondent, the intelligence of many Americas south of the Missouri and Ohio Rivers. And she wanted most of all to write about Indians. About the time that *Laughing Boy* was awarded the Pulitzer Prize, Natachee Scott went off to Oklahoma to visit Lela Ware. And there she met Lela's cousin Alfred Morris Mammedaty, who had begun, for reasons of his own, to sign his name Momaday.

My parents were married in 1933. They had no money and no prospects of having money. It was necessary for them to live at Mountain View with my father's family. The Mammedatys were often cruel to my mother. As far as they were concerned, she was an outsider who had insinuated herself into their midst, and they set out to make her life miserable. In many ways her position was not unlike that of the old captive woman Kau-au-ointy, eighty or ninety years before. And like Kau-au-ointy, too, my mother stood up to the Kiowas; it was not in her to be run over.

There are ugly stories from those days, and there are beautiful stories. My parents' courtship was a very stormy affair, and indeed their married life, extending as I write this across forty years, has been full of passion, the most wonderful and often painful intensity—and deep, rare love. When I was a child, during those years when I was caught up in the turbulence between them I had no real perception of their love for each other. That realization came to me only much later, as a kind of balm and wisdom; and it came to me, as have the other rich revelations in my life, in moments one at a time.

I weighed well over eight pounds at birth, and my mother was scarcely more than a girl at the time, and a very small one at that. Her pregnancy was extremely uncomfortable. But the Mammedatys had very little sympathy for her. In fact, they seemed determined to take every advantage of her just then, when she was especially vulnerable. At every turn they reminded her that she was an interloper, that she could expect to have no place among them. My father balked between loyalties, backed away. No doubt my mother could have purchased an easier time of it, had she been willing to do so, but it would have cost her something of her pride, and pride she would not pay. She had considerable pride—and so had my grandmother Aho, too much indeed—and no talent for compromise. It came soon to be known in the neighborhood that a domestic war was being waged at the house above Rainy Mountain Creek.

You have more nerve than sense, staying there. Why, the Kiowas have been off the warpath—what is it?—less than fifty years.
They may kill me, but they *will* not scare me.

I had nothing to say about all this at the time, of course, but there were those who feared for my_ safety as well as my mother's. A nurse in the local doctor's office insisted that my mother go to the hospital at Lawton early, and so she did, six weeks before I was born. But there were no visitors, and my mother went nearly mad with loneliness and boredom. One day a man picked her up on the highway—she was hitchhiking in her bathrobe—and drove her to Mountain View. My father was not there. Everyone was asleep except my uncle James, who was drunk.

James Mammedaty, whom I loved, was a pathetic figure of a man. I suppose that he began to drink whiskey when he was a child; it was as if he had set out as a little boy to drink himself to death, and so he did, though it took him a long time, fifty years, more or less. All the stories that I have ever heard concerning drunken Indians are concentrated for me in the memory of that sad, helpless man. When I was a boy my cousins and I used to play tricks on him. We liked to jump out at him from hiding when he was drunk, most often. How cruel this was we could not then have imagined; there is no telling what fearful figures we appeared to be in his soft, bleeding mind's eye.

> *Jimmy, Jimmy, get under the bed,*
> *Jimmy, Jimmy, your nose is all red*
> *and blue, and blue.*

A favorite trick was this: to fill an empty Bull Durham sack with dirt and present it to him, saying that we had found it. He could never, even when sober, bring himself to doubt that it was tobacco and that it was certainly a stroke of luck that it should have turned up in his hands. His disappointment when he opened it was always genuine, and it always delighted us.

When I was older I came to understand that Jimmy was a kind man, and very sick, and I tried to think well of him. It was painful to see how severely alcohol had damaged his mind and body, that he had deteriorated early into a grotesque caricature of the man he might have been. He seemed to like me above his nieces and other nephews, and he told everyone that he meant to leave me forty acres of good wheat land in his will. But in his last days, when he was utterly helpless, he was preyed upon by unscrupulous people, and I was robbed of the land, so I believe. It might have been a sad story, but I knew of his good intentions towards me, and that was worth more to me than the land.

He had got a loaded shotgun, and he was raving and blind drunk. He placed the muzzle of the gun against me in my mother's womb and threatened to shoot. I earnestly believe that my mother's quick temper, her propensity for great and sudden anger, saved her life and mine on that occasion. For she was without fear in proportion as she was angry, and she did not flinch. Rather, she called him every kind of a coward she could think of and dared him to pull the trigger. He was confounded, weaving and unable to focus his eyes, withering under a tongue-lashing that must have unbalanced him quite as much as the liquor he had consumed. Eventually my uncle Lester got out of bed and took the gun away.

And there were moments of peace and love, when my father held us in his arms.

I see: There is moonlight on the Southern Plains. I see the black trees in the north, where the river runs and my father has set out poles on the bank. When he goes before daylight with the lantern to take them up there will be catfishes on the lines, their heads flat and green and shining, and their wide mouths grinning under their whiskers. There is a whole silence on the earth—only here and there are surfaces made of sound, frogs purring at the water's edge, a rooster crowing across the distance, the river running and lapping. And the plain rolls like water in the low light; the light is like chalk on the ripples of the land; the slow, warm wind seems to ruffle the soft light, to stir it up like dust. Oklahoma shines like the moon.

7

At four o'clock on the morning of February 27, 1934, in the Kiowa and Comanche Indian Hospital at Lawton, Oklahoma, near the old stone corral at Fort Sill, where my ancestors were imprisoned in 1873 for having fled to the last buffalo range in the Staked Plains, I was delivered into the world by an elderly Indian Service doctor who entered my name on the Standard Certificate of Birth as Novarro Scotte Mammedaty ("Momaday" having first been entered, then crossed out). I have also in my possession a notarized document issued by the United States Department of the Interior, Office of Indian Affairs, Anadarko Area Office, which reads:

To whom it may concern:

This is to certify that the records of this office show that Novarro Scott Mammedaty was born February 27, 1934 at Lawton, Oklahoma and is of ⅞ degree Indian blood, as shown on the Kiowa Indian Census roll opposite Number 2035. The official Government agency records further show that his father is Alfred Mammedaty and his mother is Natachee Scott.

By Act of June 2, 1924 (43 Stat. 253), all Indians born within the territorial limits of the United States were declared to be citizens of the United States.

The first notable event in my life was a journey to the Black Hills. When I was six months old my parents took me to Devil's Tower, Wyoming, which is called in Kiowa Tsoai, "rock tree." Here are stories within stories; I want to imagine a day in the life of a man, Pohd-lohk, who gave me a name.

8

The arbor is a square frame building, cool and dark within. Two timbers, like telegraph poles, support the high, pitched roof, which is made of rafters and shingles, warped and weather-stained. Inside, on such a day as this, there are innumerable points of light at the roof, like stars, too small to admit of beams or reflections. The arbor is a place from which the sun is excluded at midday, a room that is like dawn or dusk at noon, and always there is a particular weather inside, an air that is cooler and more fluent than that of the plain, like wind in a culvert, and a deeper, more congenial shade. At times you can hear the wind, for it runs upon the walls and moans, but you cannot know it truly until you are old and have lived with it many years; so they say, who are old. It is the same wind that brings about the chinooks in the old homeland of the Kiowas to the north, the bleak winters and black springs of the whole Great Plains. It is at once the most violent and placid motion in the universe.

There is a clapboard siding to the framework. At the base it is low, rising some three feet or so from the red, earthen floor and giving way to a wide latticework and screens, an open window that encircles the great room. Here and there are certain amenities; an icebox, a cupboard, a low shelf upon which there are metal boxes and basins, shaving mugs and a mirror, a kerosene lamp and a lantern. Adjacent to the northwest corner of the room there is another, smaller block of space, the kitchen, in which there are a stone fireplace and a chimney, a grill, a cutting board, and various implements for cooking. Just now, after the noon meal, there are fragrances of spice, of boiled meat and fried bread, melons, and warm, sweet milk. Here, at this hour, in this season, you do not expect that something extraordinary will happen, only that a bird will call out in a moment, and a low wind arise, carry, and descend.

On this August day, 1934, the old man Pohd-lohk awoke before dawn. For a time he lay still in the darkness beside his wife, Tsomah, not listening to the slow, persistent sound of her breathing in sleep, but leading his mind out and away towards the center of the day. He arose quietly and drew the light, cotton blanket about his naked body, taking up his clothes, which he carried outside and placed on the edge of the porch. At the corner of the house a dog appeared, a rangy, overgrown pup, short-haired and liver-colored, wagging its tail.

43

My grandmother and I regard my father,
who casts a long shadow.

It seemed a vague epitome of the darkness; he regarded it for a moment, then let it go.

The first light appeared among the trees like smoke and crept upon the hard, bare ground at his feet, blushed upon the skyline to the north and east, where the river made a great bend and the trees grew up in a thicket in a deep crease of the bank. He peered into the dark wall of the grove in the middle distance and saw that it drew slowly upon him in the light and wavered, so it seemed, then settled back into the depths. He thought at such times that the world was centered upon him, that everything near and far must refer to him, drawing close from every quarter upon the very place where he stood. Always he loved to be out and alone in the early morning.

He shivered and huddled over upon himself, bunching the long muscles of his arms and shoulders in the blanket. He had good use of his body still, though now he moved about slowly in his age. He was a good-looking man, having been lively in his youth and closely disciplined in his prime. His body was hard and thick and grew supple in the sun; his eyes were clear and his vision keen. In his face there was reflected all the force of will and intelligence that truly defined him. His sunburned hands were fine and fluent, and with them he could still perform the intricate work of fixing beads and feathers to buckskin, and he made arrows that were precisely delicate and true.

In a moment the sun appeared, and he held his head back and closed his eyes, praying, the long, loose white hair gathering up in the peak and fold of the blanket at his neck.

A rooster crowed among the trees. It was a shrill and vibrant sound, like a cry, that carried for long moments and held like heat on the air. He opened his eyes suddenly and looked after it, but he could not determine where the creature was, and he thought of hunting, of waiting long ago in the same light (or was it a harder, bleaker light, a midwinter dawn?) and listening for such a sound, a thin cry in the distance. Once as a young man he had heard in a high wind the whimper of young wolves, hectic and hollow, and he had known at once, instinctively, where and what they were, and he went to them quietly, directly, so that there should be almost no fear on either side, singing lowly to them. They lay huddled among the rocks, three of them, shuddering with cold, their eyes closed and their fine blue fur gaping in the wind. And he shielded them for a time with his hands and wanted so much to touch them, to hold the soft warm shapes close against him, but he dared not touch them, for fear that he should leave a scent like doom upon them, and after a while he left them alone, as he had found them.

Pohd-lohk, old wolf.

He was awake now and restless. He stepped down from the porch and crossed the yard to the place where he must purify himself, a small, hide-covered framework of eighteen willows, that which is called *seidl-ku-toh*. It stood no higher than his waist, and he entered it on his hands and knees, leaving the blanket outside, and made a fire in the pit. Then, while the stones were heating, he went out again—he felt the sun flaring upon him—to get water and to breathe the last cold air of the night into his lungs.

Later in the bath, while the stones sizzled and steam rose up around him, Pohd-lohk combed out his long hair and braided it. He thought of the dead, of Kau-au-ointy, the mother of his wives, and of Mammedaty, his stepson, of others. Already indistinct in his mind, they happened upon him often now and without substance, like sudden soft winds and shadows in his dreaming, and he imagined who they were and what had happened to them, that they should have been there and then gone forever, and he thought it a strange thing,

46

their going, sad and imponderable at the center. But at the same time the thought of it filled him with wonder, and he saw what it was to be alive. Then, always, his spirit wheeled and ran away with him, out upon an endless, sunlit plain.

Afterwards: the sun was high and the air already heavy and hot. The light was not yet flat, but nearly golden in the yard, where it was broken upon the limbs and leaves of an elm and scattered on the grass and ground. Through a window he saw a magpie drop down among the shadows, gleaming as it settled in the mottled light.

Pohd-lohk began to deal with time, his old age, a restlessness. He went into his room, the room where he and Tsomah slept, and closed the door. He opened a bureau drawer and stood for a moment before it. In it were his best possessions, including a human bone, the forearm of a Crow whose name was Two Whistles. He placed the fingers of his right hand upon it—it was hard and smooth as the stones he heated for his bath—and he caught his breath, as if the bone had quickened to his touch. He removed a book and spectacles; these he kept always together, wrapped round with a red kerchief. The book, a ledgerbook which he had obtained from the Supply Office at Fort Sill, had been in his possession for many years, from the time he was a private in L Troop, Seventh Cavalry, under the command of Hugh Scott, and it meant a great deal to him. He laid his hands to it in a certain way, with precise, familiar care. It was a calendar history of the Kiowa people from 1833.

He could not remember how it was that he came to his special regard for history, or to his resolve that he, Pohd-lohk, should set it down in pictures on a page, but the book had become a serious affair in his life. In it he indicated at first events that had been recorded on an older calendar, a painted hide, then things that had been told to him by his elders or that fell within the range of his own memory.

Now that he was old, Pohd-lohk liked to look backwards in time, and although he could neither read nor write, this book was his means. It was an instrument with which he could reckon his place in the world; it was as if he could see in its yellow, brittle leaves the long swath of his coming to old age and sense in the very nature of it—the continuity of rude images in which the meaning of his racial life inhered—a force that had been set in motion at the Beginning. The calendar was a story, or the seed of a story, and it began a hundred years in the past. Beyond that, beyond the notion of a moment in 1833, there was only the unknown, a kind of prehistoric and impenetrable genesis, a realm of no particular shape, duration, or meaning. It was an older, larger story, a story of another people, another reality at last. He believed in it, but he could not take hold of it and set it down. The Kiowas had entered the world through a hollow log; they had known good things and bad, triumph and defeat; and they had journeyed a long way from the mouth of the log. But it was all one moment to Pohd-lohk, as if everything, the whole world, had been created on an afternoon in 1830 or 1832.

He opened the book to the first page, and it was *Da-pegya-de Sai,* November, 1833, and the stars were falling. He closed his eyes, the better to see them. They were everywhere in the darkness, so numerous and bright indeed that the night was shattered. They flew like sparks, he thought, and he thought also of slender, pointed leaves turning in the sun, and of pure light glittering upon water. But as he watched, dreaming, the stars were at last like nothing he had ever seen or should ever see beyond this, the havoc he imagined and remembered in his blood. Truly they were not like sparks or leaves or facets of light upon water. In some older and more nearly perfect synthesis of motion and light the stars wheeled across the vision of his mind's eye. They swung and veered; they drew near and loomed; and they fell slowly and silently away in the void. Silently. Men, women, and children were running here and there in the flashing light, their eyes wide and their mouths twisted with fear, but he could not hear their running, nor even the sound of their cries. And yet it did not seem strange to him that there should be no sound upon the scene. It was as if the earth—or even so much of it as he knew—had fallen off into the still, black depths. Even as this bright catastrophe was somehow the element of his perception just now, in his dreaming, so was silence the element in which the stars moved inexorably. They fell in long arcs and traces, bright delineations of time and space, describing eternity. He looked after them with strange exhilaration, straining to see.

Or it was *Ta'dalkop Sai*, 1839–40, and the designation before him was the crude figure of a man covered with red spots. This was in commemoration of the great smallpox epidemic which began on the upper Missouri in the summer of 1837 and which, in the course of three years, is estimated to have destroyed fully one third of the native inhabitants of the Great Plains.

Always when he thought of it Pohd-lohk could see the bodies of the dead, not their faces, but only their faceless forms, the abstractions of some hideous reality that was a shade beyond his comprehension. More real to him by far were the survivors, those whose grief, he thought, must have been a plague in itself, whose wailing must have been like the drone of locusts in the fields. In his own lifetime, 1892, he had seen a woman kneeling over the body of her child, who had succumbed to measles. She had inflicted bloody wounds upon her arms and shoulders with a knife; she had cut her hair so that it lay close to the scalp and ragged. And all the while that he watched, his rage and shame having come together in a kind of helpless fascination, she emitted cries, hollow, thin, full of wild, incomprehensible grief.

Again, it was 1851–52. That winter there was a hard thing for the coming-out people to bear. A Pawnee boy who had been captured the year before by Set-angya, the great warrior chief of the Kaitsenko society, escaped and took with him the best horse in the tribe, a bay hunter known as Guadal-tseyu, "Little Red." Pohd-lohk had turned this matter over in his mind a thousand times. It might have been a different story among the Pawnees, the story of the boy. But in his own terms, which comprised Pohd-lohk's particular idea of history, it was the story of the horse—and incidentally of the Kiowas at a given moment in time. Moreover, it was a tragic story—nearly as much so from his point of view as was that of the plague, which he imagined no more vividly—inasmuch as it centered upon a whole and crucial deprivation, the loss of a horse, a hunting horse, a loss that involved the very life's blood of the culture. Once upon a time, as he thought of it, there was a horse, and never before had there been such a horse, and it was lost, and with it was lost something of the coming-out people, too, a splinter from the bone. It was a simple story in the telling, but there were many implications, many shadows on the grass. He imagined Guadal-tseyu. Now and then it seemed to him that he had got hold of it, that he could feel the horse under him, the whole strength and whole motion of it. It was hard to hold and half wild in its spirit, but it was all the more congenial to his mind for that, all the more appropriate to the landscape from which it had sprung like a gust of wind. He thought he could see it, the red hunting horse, but it was fleeting. He saw the ghost, the sheer energy of it. Perhaps when it stood still, he thought, it was the ordinary image of a horse, neither more nor less, standing away in the whole hollow of the plain, or away on a ridge, the sky all around it, small and alone, lonely. But when it wheeled and broke into a run, as it did always in his dreaming, it seemed to concentrate the wind and the stars, to gather the splinters of the sun to itself. And someone in his lineage, a man long ago in the Yellowstone, had seen such a thing, a fish flashing at a waterfall in the late afternoon, hurtling high above a dark rainbow on the spray.

Or it was the summer of 1883, in which Sampt'e was killed. Pohd-lohk had known this man and had seen fit to commemorate him, to fix him forever in the scheme of remembered time. But now, as he thought back to that green summer, it was the sun dance that stood out in his mind. It was called *A'dalk'atoi K'ado*, "Nez Percé sun dance." Pohd-lohk was in his twenties at the time. He was then, as he thought of it now, at the end of his youth, as vital and strong as he should ever be, and scarcely concerned to admit of age or illness. *A'dalk'atoi K'ado.* He thought of it as the one time in his life to which he would willingly return from any and all other times; it was simply the best of his memories. The place of the sun dance was pasture land by that time, owned and enclosed by a white cattleman whom the Kiowas called Map'odal, "Split-nose." The lodge was erected on a low rise of dark, rich land on the Washita River where two dense groves of pecan trees grew in a large semicircle. It was a bright, hot summer, a summer of the plains, and it followed upon a hard winter. The camps were gleaming against the dark, shimmering backdrop of the groves, and the arbors, faceted with bright leaves, shone like fire, and there were pennants of red and blue and yellow cloth everywhere, moving in the breeze.

That summer the Nez Percés came. It was then five years since they had been released from imprisonment at Fort Leavenworth and two before they should be allowed to return to their northern homeland. They seemed a regal people, as tall as the Kiowas, as slow to reveal themselves. There was an excitement about them, something of legendary calm and courage. It was common knowledge that, under their great chief Joseph, they had fought brilliantly against the United States and had come very close to victory. It was the first time that Pohd-lohk had seen them, but he had known of them all his life. The Kiowas remembered that, long ago, they had come upon these imposing people, "people with hair cut off across the forehead," in the highlands on the edge of the Northern Plains. This was a part of that larger story in which Pohd-lohk believed. It was a good thing to have the Nez Percés; they were worthy guests, worthy of him, he thought, of his youthful vigor and good looks. For their benefit he strutted about and set his mouth just so, in the attitude of a warrior.

And there were Tsomah and Keahdinekeah, whom he would take for his wives. Keahdinekeah was then twenty-five years old and the mother of the child Mammedaty. She was slender and straight, and she had inherited her mother Kau-au-ointy's strength of will and character. She carried herself with remarkable dignity and grace, so much so indeed that these traits should be apparent even to a child, her great-grandson, sixty years later.

Pohd-lohk sang, for a man sings of such a woman. His dreaming came to an end in the song, and he put the book and spectacles away. His mind turned and drew upon something else now, something that had run through his thoughts for several days, a serious matter. It was time to go, and he set out, walking easily in the heat, towards the trees that grew on Rainy Mountain Creek.

There, in a wide clearing above the bank, Keahdinekeah sat on the edge of the bed in her room. It was late morning, almost noon, and she had been sitting there alone for a long time. It was very hot; even though the window was wide open, the air was heavy and stale in the room. The room smelled of old, settled things, curios and keepsakes that were Keahdinekeah's, having no essence but that of belonging to her. She nodded from time to time, dozing, her eyes closed and her small, crooked hands folded in her lap. She was very small, as if in her waning and weariness all of her little, aged bones had collapsed within her. She was seventy-six years old now, and nearly blind. Unlike Pohd-lohk, she showed her age, seemed even older than she was. Since the death of Mammedaty, her firstborn and favorite son, she had withdrawn into herself—in grief at first, but then as a matter of preference. She had finished with the things that enabled her to live well in the ordinary world; they had passed away from her one by one; and now she was herself waiting to pass away into the darkness that had come upon her and lay like evening at her eyes. It was a long wait—and it would go on for more than a decade—but she kept it with trust and good will. And she was glad to have visitors when they came.

Without knocking, Pohd-lohk opened the door to her room. She looked up, but he knew that she could not see who was there.

Old woman.
Old man!

He paused for a moment in the doorway, wiping the sweat from his forehead.

It is hot.
Yes?
Hot.

There was a dull luster upon the objects in the room, the knobs of metal and hollows of wood, the blocks and wedges of a patchwork quilt, bits of carnival glass. There was a very low amber brilliance, a soft, nearly vibrant glowing, upon the whole setting. The air was close, stifling.

Come, old woman, let's sit outside, in the arbor.

She held out her hand to him, and he helped her to stand and walk. They went out of the house and across the yard, where a speckled hen scratched in the dirt beside a shallow cistern at the well.

It raised its head and regarded them sideways. Keahdinekeah walked
very softly, in moccasins, on Pohd-lohk's arm.

The arbor was a makeshift affair, nothing but a lean-to, made out
of poles and branches. The poles were many years old, smooth and
gray, with long, gaping cracks here and there. The branches had been
placed on the framework in May or June; the leaves had long since
wilted, and most of them were shriveled now and brittle, in spite of
the very humid heat. Even so, the arbor afforded them a little shade,
and it was soothing. They sat down on a bench at the long table, over
the top of which a heavy red oilcloth had been stretched and tacked
down. It was ragged and badly faded, but it was cool to the touch.
Flies buzzed about them, slowly, as if they were moving against a
wind.

How is my sister Tsomah?
Oh, she is all right, very well, in fact. She said to tell you that she
is drying some meat, that you ought to come and pay her a visit.
Yes? Well, it may be so, but I don't get out much, you know. I
can't see very well at all now.

She looked straight ahead, her eyes open, and he could see in them
the milky film of her blindness. A silence fell between them, and she
reached for his hand, held it tight, smiling.

Well, Pohd-lohk, it is good to have you here; I am glad that you
came.
So, I must go on about my business.
Yes?
It is very important.
Yes?
Oh, yes.
Well, then.

54

I am on my way to see your great-grandson.
Eh neh neh neh neh!

She clasped her hands together, laughing. And after a moment she was lost in thought, and again there was a silence between them.

And afterwards, when Pohd-lohk had gone, Keahdinekeah sat again on the edge of her bed and thought of Tsoai and of her great-grandson. Neither had she ever seen, but of Tsoai she knew an old story.

Eight children were there at play, seven sisters and their brother. Suddenly the boy was struck dumb; he trembled and began to run upon his hands and feet. His fingers became claws, and his body was covered with fur. There was a bear where the boy had been. The sisters were terrified; they ran, and the bear after them. They came to the stump of a great tree, and the tree spoke to them. It bade them climb upon it, and as they did so it began to rise into the air. The bear came to kill them, but they were just beyond its reach. It reared against the tree and scored the bark all around with its claws. The seven sisters were borne into the sky, and they became the stars of the Big Dipper.

Tsoai loomed in her mind; nor could she have imagined it more awesome than it is, the great black igneous monolith that rises out of the Black Hills of Wyoming to a height of twelve hundred feet above the Belle Fourche River. Many generations before, the Kiowas had come upon Tsoai, had been obliged in their soul to explain it to themselves. And they imagined that it stood in some strange and meaningful relation to them and to the stars. It was therefore a sacred thing, Keahdinekeah knew. And her grandson Huan-toa had taken his child to be in Tsoai's presence even before the child could understand what it was, so that by means of the child the memory of Tsoai should be renewed in the blood of the coming-out people. Of this she thought, and she said to herself: Yes, old man, I see; I see now what your errand is.

Pohd-lohk crossed Rainy Mountain Creek on a log, a walnut that he himself had felled the year before. The trees were thick along the creek, the foliage dense. There were shafts of sunlight all about, smoking, so many planes of bright light on the dark shadows of the creek. Birds fluttered up here and there, flashing across the planes and angles of light in the tunnel of trees. Insects made minute, hectic motions on the brown water, which bore up a long, crooked drift, the most fragile mesh of silt and webs. Small white butterflies glittered and bobbed in the humid air, moving in their own way, rising and falling in time to a rhythm too intricate for the old man to follow with his eyes. It was like a dance. He picked his way along a dim, narrow path that led upwards through brier and berry thickets to the top of the land.

Ahead on the highest knoll was the house where Mammedaty had lived in his last years, the arbor and the barn. These, from where he walked now on the first wave of the plain above the creek, stood up against the sky, as if they were the only landmarks in a hundred miles. In the conjugation of distance and light at this hour of the day they might have been little or large, near or far away. It seemed to him that he was forever coming upon them.

In the arbor Pohd-lohk entered among the members of his dead stepson's family and was full of good humor and at ease. He took up the child in his hands and held it high, and he cradled it in his arms, singing to it and rocking it to and fro. With the others he passed the time of day, exchanged customary talk, scattered small exclamations on the air: Yes, yes. Quite so. So it is with us. But with the child he was deliberate, intent. And after a time all the other voices fell away, and his own grew up in their wake. It became monotonous and incessant, like a long running of the wind. The whole of the afternoon was caught up in it and carried along. Pohd-lohk spoke, as if telling a story, of the coming-out people, of their long journey. He spoke of how it was that everything began, of Tsoai, and of the stars falling or holding fast in strange patterns on the sky. And in this, at last, Pohd-lohk affirmed the whole life of the child in a name, saying: Now you are, Tsoai-talee.

I am. It is when I am most conscious of being that wonder comes upon my blood, and I want to live forever, and it is no matter that I must die.

Five generations. Kau-au-ointy, Keah-dinekeah, Mammeaaty, Clara, and Marland.

TWO

1

IN MY EARLIEST years I traveled a number of times from Oklahoma to the Navajo reservation in New Mexico and Arizona and back again. The two landscapes are fixed in my mind. They are separate realities, but they are sometimes confused in my memory. I place my feet in the plain, but my prints are made on the mountain.

I was much alone. I had no brothers or sisters, and as it happened in my childhood, much of it, my peers were at removes from me, across cultures and languages. I had to create my society in my mind. And for a child this kind of creation is accomplished easily enough. I imagined much.

When I was three years old my head must have been full of Indian as well as English words. The sounds of both Kiowa and Navajo are quite natural and familiar to me, and even now I can make these sounds easily and accurately with my voice, so well established are they in my ear. I lived very close to these "foreign" languages, poised at a crucial time in the learning process to enter into either or both of them wholly. But my mother was concerned that I should learn English as my "native" language, and so English is first and foremost in my possession. My mother's love of books, and of English literature in particular, is intense, and naturally she wanted me to share in it. I have seen Grendel's shadow on the walls of Canyon de Chelly, and once, having led the sun around Hoskinini Mesa, I saw Copperfield at Oljeto Trading Post.

In 1936 Haske Noswood, a Navajo friend, invited my parents and me to come to Gallup, New Mexico, where my mother and father hoped to find work in the Indian Service. We arrived at the time of Naa'ahoohai, the old celebration of the Navajos which had by that time become the Intertribal Indian Ceremonial. The Navajos came from far and wide to Gallup, which is called in Navajo Na'nizhoozhi, the "place of the bridge" on the Rio Puerco. We lived in the Del Mar Hotel, across from the old Harvey House on the Santa Fe Railroad, and I slept in a bureau drawer. My father found a temporary job: he painted signs for the traders in the Ceremonial exhibit hall at fifty cents a sign. And later he got on as a truck dispatcher with the Roads Department, Indian Service, at Shiprock, which is called in Navajo Naat'aaniineez (literally "tall chief"; the town takes its name from the great monolith that stands nearby in an arid reach of the San Juan Basin). The name Shiprock, like other Anglicizations in this region, seems incongruous enough, but from certain points of view—and from the air, especially—the massive rock Naat'aaniineez resembles very closely a ship at sea. Soon thereafter my mother was offered the job of switchboard operator at Shiprock Agency, which she accepted, and we were a solvent and independent entity. My parents have told me time and again what an intoxication were those days, and I think back to them on that basis; they involve me in a tide of confidence and well-being. What on earth was not possible? I must have been carried along in the waves of hope and happiness that were gathered in the hearts of my young and free and beautiful parents.

In the years between 1936 and 1943 we lived on the Navajo reservation at Shiprock, New Mexico, and at Tuba City, then Chinle, Arizona. There were in that span of time a number of sojourns away from home—to Oklahoma, to Kentucky, even to Louisiana (where my aunt Ethel lived at the time), and for several months my mother and I, while my father waited in Oklahoma to be drafted into the army (it turned out that he wasn't drafted, though the war was raging then), lived on the San Carlos Apache reservation in the southeastern quadrant of Arizona—but "home" was particularly the Navajo country, Dine bikeyah. My earliest playmates and schoolmates were Navajo children and the children of Indian Service employees. Just at the time I was learning to talk, I heard the Navajo language spoken all around me. And just as I was coming alive to the wide world, the vast and beautiful landscape of Dine bikeyah *was* my world, all of it that I could perceive.

Memory begins to qualify the imagination, to give it another formation, one that is peculiar to the self. I remember isolated, yet fragmented and confused, images—and images, shifting, enlarging, is the word, rather than moments or events—which are mine alone and which are especially vivid to me. They involve me wholly and immediately, even though they are the disintegrated impressions of a young child. They call for a certain attitude of belief on my part now; that is, they must mean something, but their best reality does not consist in meaning. They are not stories in that sense, but they are storylike, mythic, never evolved but evolving ever. There are such things in the world: it is in their nature to be believed; it is not

61

The horse is Tony. I am being pursued.

necessarily in them to be understood. Of all that must have happened to and about me in those my earliest days, why should these odd particulars alone be fixed in my mind? If I were to remember other things, I should be someone else.

There is a room full of light and space. The walls are bare; there are no windows or doors of which I am aware. I am inside and alone. Then gradually I become aware of another presence in the room. There is an object, something not extraordinary at first, something of the room itself—but what I cannot tell. The object does not matter at first, but at some point—after a moment? an hour?—it moves, and I am unsettled. I am not yet frightened; rather I am somewhat surprised, vaguely anxious, fascinated, perhaps. The object grows; it expands farther and farther beyond definition. It is no longer an object but a mass. It is so large now that I am dwarfed by it, reduced almost to nothing. And *now* I am afraid, nearly terrified, and yet I have no will to resist; I remain attentive, strangely curious in proportion as I am afraid. The huge, shapeless mass is displacing all of the air, all of the space in the room. It swells against me. It is soft and supple and resilient, like a great bag of water. At last I am desperate, desperately afraid of being suffocated, lost in some dimple or fold of this vague, enormous thing. I try to cry out, but I have no voice.

Restore my voice for me.

How many times has this memory been nearly recovered, the definition almost realized! Again and again I have come to that awful edge, that one word, perhaps, that I cannot bring from my mouth. I sometimes think that it is surely a name, the name of someone or something, that if only I could utter it, the terrific mass would snap away into focus, and I should see and recognize what it is at once; I should have it then, once and for all, in my possession.

It is a bright, hot day, but the arbor is cool. The smooth gray wood of the benches is cool to the touch. The worn patchwork covers are cool and soft. The red, hard-packed earth of the floor is dark and cool. It is quiet and sleepy inside. I love this place. I love the cool well water that I bring in a dipper to my mouth.

One time the creek was backed up, and my dad . . .
Was it that time he saw the animal, the . . .
Yes, that was it; that was the time.

We set out, my father and I, in the afternoon. We walk down the long grade to the ravine that runs diagonally below, up again and through the brambles. The sun burns my skin. I feel the stiff spines and furry burrs at my legs and hear the insects humming there all around. We walk down into the shadows of Rainy Mountain Creek. The banks are broad and the mud is dry and cracked, broken into innumerable large facets like shards of pottery, smooth, delicately curved, where the water has risen and then withdrawn and the sun has baked the bank. The water is brown and runs very slowly at the surface; here and there are glints of light and beams that strike through the trees and splash on the rocks and roots and underbrush. We cross the creek on a log and climb up the west bank where the woods are thicker. There is a small clearing, and inside the clearing is a single tree that was bent down to the ground and tied as a sapling; and so it remains curved, grown over in a long, graceful arc, its nimble new branches brushing whorls on the ground. It is one of my delights, for it is a wonderful, lively swing. My father lifts me up and I take hold of the slender, tapered trunk, and then he pulls me down and lets me go. I spring up, laughing, laughing, and bob up and down.

64

We continue on, through fields now, to "across the creek," as the house there was always called when I was a child. It is Keahdinekeah's house, built for her by my grandfather; but when you are a child you don't think of houses as possessions; it does not occur to you that anyone has ownership in them. "Across the creek" is where Justin Lee lives, a cousin not much older than I, with his sister, Lela, and his parents, Jim and Dorothy Ware, and his grandmother Keahdinekeah.

It seems reasonable to suppose that I visited my great-grandmother on other occasions, but I remember only this once, and I remember it very well. My father leads me into her room. It is dark and close inside, and I cannot see until my eyes become accustomed to the dim light. There is a certain odor in the room and not elsewhere in the house, the odor of my great-grandmother's old age. It is not unpleasant, but it is most particular and exclusive, as much hers as is her voice or her hair or the nails of her hands. Such a thing has not only the character of great age but something also of the deep self, of one's own dignity and well-being. Because of this, I believe, this old blind woman is like no one I have ever seen or shall ever see. To a child her presence is formidable. My father is talking to her in Kiowa, and I do not understand what is being said, only that the talk is of me. She is seated on the side of her bed, and my father brings me to stand directly in front of her. She reaches out for me and I place my hands in hers. *Eh neh neh neh neh.* She begins to weep very softly in a high, thin, hollow voice. Her hands are little and soft, so soft that they seem not to consist in flesh and bone, but in the softest fiber, cotton or fine wool. Her voice is so delicate, so surely expressive of her deep feelings. Long afterwards I think: That was a wonderful and beautiful thing that happened in my life. There, on that warm, distant afternoon: an old woman and a child, holding hands across the generations. There is great good in such a remembrance; I cannot imagine that it might have been lost upon me.

65

Lester and I, when we were little, used to go to my aunt's house in a wagon.

Where?

She lived over by the Wichitas; I thought of it as being far away.

Was it far away?

I thought so. At night we heard wolves in the mountains.

I am lying in bed beside an open window in the house. The room is dark, and the moonlight is brilliant on the yard outside. Everything is recessed in those marvelous blue depths of the summer night; the grass and the leaves glisten. The arbor is white and gleaming across the way, the screens black and opaque until someone inside strikes a match, and the little flame, set away in that darkness, is intensely bright for a moment, then gone out; and then a cigarette glows there, now and then visible. On such evenings the family sits there in the arbor without lamps, letting the night take hold of them, savoring the cool air. But in the house it is warm. It would be uncomfortably warm were it not for that same most delicate breeze that steals in at the window. It is impossible to say how clean and delicious it is. I hear voices from the arbor, low, monotonous, indistinct—and now and again laughter; there are crickets and frogs across the range of the night, everywhere, nowhere. And at long intervals I hear trucks passing along the highway on the south side of the house, in the red cut of the knoll, the high-pitched singing of the tires. There is something unspeakably lonely in that sound, and in that respect it is like the faraway whistle of a train, or the wind at Keet Seel. It is so familiar to me, a sound which seems to pervade my memory of those Indian evenings in Oklahoma; and yet I think it has nothing to do with me, after all; it might as well be the whir of a star moving across infinity. The door opens and the room flares up in yellow light; around the walls slivers of shadows leap to the lamp in my grandmother's hand. She places the lamp on a bureau, looses her long braids, dresses for bed. And then she prays aloud in Kiowa, standing, her eyes closed tight in concentration and earnestness. Her voice goes on and on; it is strange-sounding, rich, rhythmical, hypnotic. I try to hold on to it, to stay awake inside it, but I slip away at last into sleep. I awaken, and the voice, my father's voice, laps softly against my mind:

and the man went on in the same way, pointing the arrow all around

and it is warm in the bed, under heavy blankets, and there is a taut wind at the windows, and the winter is coming on. Deer are huddled in the Carizos; horses are braced against the cold at Lukachukai.

Dawn is on the desert for a long time, and the air is clean and cold; it feels like frost, and it draws the skin tight about the hands and face. Look across the dunes wrinkled with light and shadow; the colors, before they deepen, are the colors of shells or of birds' eggs.

My father is at the wheel of a new green pickup, and I am sitting beside him, hugely pleased to be along. The dashboard is gray-brown and to me very beautiful; there are bright knobs in it. My father is wearing gloves, soft leather gloves, and that is unimaginably fine. My dog Blackie is at the rear window, riding high to the wind, looking, laughing in at me. I look out in every direction to see who will notice us, for we are wonderful to behold, speeding along in the new truck, handsome, handsome, our eyes glittering; and otherwise, too, there is so much to see; the wide world is enchanted. The little truck bounces over the dirt roads of the Navajo reservation, raises a great rooster tail of red dust. It is summer and there is a sharp glare on the sand, on the cottonwood leaves. There is a jolt which rattles my bones, and the buckboard bucks; snowflakes are whirling on the sharp wind. My mother and I hold on, on the way to Oraibi. The old man sitting above us is wearing gloves; he talks to the team and crouches in his

67

striped blanket. I am freezing. Then there is a mug of coffee, steaming, in my mother's hands. She holds it out to me and I take it in both my hands and bring it to my lips. It is black and bitter and good, better to hold than to taste. Perhaps it is my first taste of coffee. The sky is bleak and immense, streaked with smoke. I not only hear the beat of the drums; I feel it, too, and I feel the voices of the singers. It is a particular music which touches me, moves inside me like my blood. I listen. The whistle moans and the engine swerves ahead and the cars lurch and whine on the rails, rolling on the long, horizontal axis, shifting under me. I go here and there, back and forth, on trains. I am known by sight to the crews of the Santa Fe; the nurse on the *Scout* looks out for me. One man, a wily black, crooked as a hairpin, comes to stop my crying. He tells me that children who cry on the train are put in a sack and dropped off at Winslow. His uniform glitters with bits of brass.

A wiry old man comes out of the trading post at Tuba City. Squatting, he opens a can of whole tomatoes with a knife; he pours sugar from a sack, a lot of it, on the tomatoes and eats them from the can, with his knife. He has a good belt, old plaques. Nizhoni yei!

Monument Valley: red to blue; great violent shadows, planes and prisms of light. Once, from a window in the wall of a canyon, I saw men on horseback, far below, two of them, moving slowly into gloaming, and they were singing. They were so far away that I could only barely see them, and their small, clear voices lay very lightly and for a long time on the distance between us.

The valley is vast. When you look out over it, it does not occur to you that there is an end to it. You see the monoliths that stand away in space, and you imagine that you have come upon eternity. They do not appear to exist in time. You think: I see that time comes to an end on this side of the rock, and on the other side there is nothing

68

Tsoai of my name, Tsoai-talee

forever. I believe that only in *dine bizaad*, the Navajo language, which is endless, can this place be described, or even indicated in its true character. Just there is the center of an intricate geology, a whole and unique landscape which includes Utah, Colorado, Arizona, and New Mexico. The most brilliant colors in the earth are there, I believe, and the most beautiful and extraordinary land forms—and surely the coldest, clearest air, which is run through with pure light.

The long wall of red rocks which extends eastward and for miles from Gallup, New Mexico, describes something of the hard, bright beauty of the continent at its summit. The Continental Divide runs down and intersects this wall at Coolidge. In the long reach of country which lies between Coolidge and the red rock wall there are cattle and sheep, rabbits and roadrunners, all delightful to a child. And there are trains. In the middle distance is the Santa Fe Railroad. Trains, most often long, slow-going freight trains, move there, one after another without end—and so they moved there when I was a child. They were small and nearly silent in the distance, and they bore upon the land in an easy, nearly discreet way. They seemed not to intrude, that is, as machines do in so many of the landscapes of our time; or perhaps this is merely *my* sense of things, having long ago taken that countryside as I found it, cut through with glinting rails and puffing trains. Like the red wall above them, they made an ordinary stratum on the scene. I try to imagine that large expanse without them, but then there is a flaw in the design. For in my mind's eye, too, a train stitches black across the plain.

Gallup is a rough-edged town of dubious character and many surfaces of rich color. It is a place of high tensions and hard distinctions. I once heard someone say that Gallup is the last frontier town in America; there is a certain truth to that, I believe. On a given day you can see in the streets of Gallup cowboys and Indians, missionaries and miscreants, tradesmen and tourists. Or you can see Billy the Kid or Huckleberry Finn or Ganado Mucho—or someone who is not impossibly all these worthies in one, Everyman realized in some desperate notion of himself.

To the child I was in the thirties Gallup was a wonderful, enchanted city, wonderful in its high tones and wide motions, wonderful in its din and audacity. It was almost too much for a child to take in, a child who had come fresh from the deep interior of the reservation. Gleaming automobiles passed endlessly along Route 66; mammoth, steaming locomotives drew up at the Harvey House; covered wagons rolled along the Rio Puerco. And there was a fabulous booty in the store windows! I can still feel the child's excitement of that place. Years afterwards, in the ancient city of Samarkand, in the

I believe that I was thinking
on great things.

old bazaar there, I had precisely the same *gladness* in me that I had when I was a child come on a Saturday morning from Naat'aaniineez to Na'nizhoozhi.

2

The sun was going down, and now the sky was red and purple in the west. For a few minutes the buildings of the town of Mountain View were edged with orange light, especially the underside of a water tank and the white wall of a silo; then the buildings backed off into the dusk and there was a blur upon them. The panes of a window in Mammedaty's house caught the last glare of the sun.

The darkness rose like a flood from the creek, and there was nothing in it, only a kind of long, lateral hush that divided the plain. It rose, but it could not be seen to rise; it could be seen only to hold off. A spotted cat came out from under the south porch of Mammedaty's house, regarded something with its head slung low, and returned. The air told time.

James sat at the oval table in the dining room with his young nephew, muttering sometimes under his breath, as he did always and for no apparent reason, and his mother brought a platter of meat and eggs from the kitchen. The light had gone out of the room, and James struck a match and set fire to the wick in the lamp. When the globe was set down upon it the flame grew hard and bright, but for a time it seemed not to make much of a difference in the color—it was one color—of the room.

The boy, whose first home this was, was homesick. He suffered intensely, knowing that his grandmother and his uncle were watching him. They did not want him to cry. He thought it over; he wanted to cry. Earlier, in the afternoon, when he had played out his solitary games and gone almost to sleep while sitting on a log, watching, listening, rather, to his uncle chop wood, he had cried. A loneliness had grown up in him, and he could no longer keep it all to himself. But at the same time he was ashamed to cry, and so he cried in spite of himself, blinking the tears hard from his eyes, giving no more voice to his crying than he could help.

James cut up some meat on the boy's plate and pushed the plate across the table to the boy's place. There was a blue floral design all around the rim of the white plate, and the pieces of meat were nearly black in the lamplight, and the eggs were fried hard and edged with a thin brown crust, and they were shiny with grease. His grandmother poured the boy some milk from a gray metal pitcher into a tumbler of carnival glass; little bunches of grapes were raised in the glass, lightly frosted with blue and purple. Then she sat down between the boy and his uncle and prayed. She ended with the words, "in Jesus' name. Amen." These were the only words the boy understood.

The boy tried to eat, but he had no appetite, and so after a few minutes he could take nothing but the milk. The milk was warm and fresh and very sweet, having come only a little while before from one of the leaseman's cows. The boy had watched the milking, had patted the cow's shoulder as it stood at the trough in Mammedaty's barn, had seen the thin streams of white milk spurting into the pail. He had been fascinated. "Where you from?" the leaseman said. "Shiprock," the boy answered. "Where's that?" But the boy had forgotten where Shiprock was, and he was suddenly, painfully embarrassed. "Texas?" the leaseman offered. "No." "Kansas? Nebraska?" "No." "Illinois, Missouri, Ohio?" "Maybe Missouri," the boy said. He knew that was wrong, but he had to get out of this predicament. "Yes, Missouri," he said absolutely. "Huh. Ain't never been there," the leaseman said.

73

Affable, I sit in the yard at Mountain View. Old people came there to pay their respects. I have seen them in the yard.

And the boy had played in Mammedaty's barn, among the stalls in the wet, stinking straw, stirring up the dust, the dry alfalfa dust, until his clothes were full of chaff and manure and dust, and his grandmother had to take his clothes and shake them out and wash them, and he had to sit in an old galvanized washtub in the kitchen in gray, soapy water in which his grandmother poured more and more hot water from a great kettle on the old wood stove. And he had seen a box of bones in the barn and had been afraid to touch them, but he touched them anyway. They were the bones of a horse, *Guadal-tseyu.*

The boy's grandmother leased most of the land out, now that Mammedaty was gone, and the income was substantial. There was a good deal of land, and much of it was clear and fertile. James, too, had good land of his own, some of the richest land in the state. The leasemen were always trying to buy the land, but neither Aho nor James would sell it. James had received some lease money that day. Had his nephew been older and known what money was, James would have given him some, a generous amount, even, as he would do many times in the years to come, for the satisfaction. The man loved the boy.

The boy held the milk up to the lamp and looked through the carnival glass. His grandmother and his uncle scolded him for not eating, but he knew that he could have his way, and he pleaded simply that he was not hungry and went on playing with the glass. He felt better, and he was getting sleepy.

Well anyway I have this gun this real-looking gun black and brown smooth and hard a carbine tomorrow I will shoot an Indian down by the creek he will see me but I will see him first and I will wait until he sees me it has to be that way of course he sees me and of course he is surprised his eyes are big and his mouth is open and he is *ugly* of course he has a knife it is a great big knife and it gleams and

75

flashes in the sunlight it was stolen of course oh I know that good
knife it was stolen from my grandfather one night when he left it
outside by the arbor where he liked to cut meat he talked about it of
course he meant to give it to my father and my father meant to give
it to me it is really my knife the ugly Indian sees me and I am
looking right at him and I have been looking right at him for a long
long time he recognizes me of course it has to be that way he has
been afraid of me all these years running and hiding from me and
now it has come to this he is famous because of the knife he has of
course killed many men women and children with the knife and he is
called Knife sometimes Big Knife sometimes Knife Thrower then after
a moment he smiles and he is even uglier so it is you at last he says
and I nod there is a moment between us then he makes his lightning
move and the knife is wheeling in the air and of course I shoot him
and nimbly nimbly I catch the knife in the stock of my gun over my
heart and the ugly Indian staggers and slumps and pitches headfirst
into a ravine and I say you're dead and of course it is so

The cow was a pretty thing her shoulders were warm and smooth
and so soft to touch the color of moccasins

I saw too a very fat man with no neck just a black line between his
head and shoulders his teeth and the nails of his huge hands were the
same color what color a pretty little girl yellow and thin a dirty baby
waddling linoleum broken somewhere a dead dog grinning on the side
of the road the flies all over it rabbits other guns none as good as the
carbine a white radio in the window of Crabtree's drugstore the back
of the leaseman's red neck silt moving on the creek an anthill the
head of Jesus Christ in a cloud a jar of jellybeans many of them black
a green tractor my uncle's stomach through his shirt the teats of the
moccasin-colored cow

Grandma and Jimmy in the next room talking sometimes funny words I don't know what they are all of them I know one or two words here and there now and then the talk is so slow there are long silences

There are long silences in which dishes rattle, pots and pans ring. Then there is talk, slow, emphatic. I turn over on my stomach, holding the carbine close against me, at the ready. There is a line of light under the door, not a line, really, but a long, thin triangle of light, under the door. The talk is there in that splinter of light, sliding along, now . . . now . . . now, now sharp, now muffled, close, distant, drawing away, and the black at the window going to blue within my reach. Somewhere a syllable draws away, and a breeze slants across the night, and there is nothing else.

James was slouched at the oval table, his right arm lying under his absent gaze on the oilcloth, his right hand hanging down from the edge, the fingers curled slightly, the thumb extended almost to his left thigh, his head hanging. And across the table sat Aho, his mother, composed, her hands interlaced in her lap, her feet crossed. Her eyes, partly closed and downcast, shone in the lamplight, and she was chewing gum. In her pensive moments she almost always chewed gum, slowly, exactly, as if, with her back teeth, to regulate her thoughts.

James thought of the boy, his nephew. It was his concession to the boy that he had seen him through the day, had led him around the empty spaces of time in the morning and afternoon, especially the late afternoon, when the shadows stood still. They had walked down to the town, had looked into the wide street, had carried out their business like men of the world, in the post office, in the bank, had eaten ice cream, had bought the good toy gun. They had gone along together, or their paths had crossed many times through the day.

Through the day. The day had come down to the night, and the boy was asleep, safe and sound. Now:

A knot was being drawn very tight inside the man. The thought, just the thought, of being drunk had a physical effect upon him, a giddiness, a kind of euphoria in which his body seemed to grow lighter and more supple, and at the same time there was a kind of resistance in it, in the flesh and blood, the body's own anticipation of impairment and pain, of dehydration and the sharp contraction of the brain. His eyes went very dry—and his tongue—and sweat broke out at his head and at the palms of his hands.

He saw his mother out of the corner of his eye. Aho did not provoke him, except that the patience in her pressed upon him like a weariness. It lay between them as a long distance or an interval that he could not comprehend. She was entirely composed. A painter should have loved her in her composure then, in the lamplight. Momently the light shivered in her hair, so lowly that it seemed barely to emanate there. Her head, her face, her shoulders, her bosom were ample and round. Nothing, neither the corners of her eyes and mouth, nor the folds of her flesh and the shadows that were set upon her, hardened to an edge or an angle or a flatness anywhere. Her skin was dark, and yet her face was so radiant against the shadows and the deeper darkness of her hair and her dress that her whole expression was laid out and defined there, fashioned upon the broad, round bone of her skull, which was prominent just now in the strange quality of the light. Her eyes were half-closed, and neither did the lamp's reflection which guttered there seem any way hard and precise, but soft and transparent. The painter should have wondered how to indicate such a thing. He should have had to work a great illusion into a single point, something more a matter of texture than of color, perhaps. He should have had to bring his artist's hand and his artist's eye so close together as to be one and the same thing. She seemed

78

very wise and very strong, and her strength seemed to consist in rest. She seemed simply to know how to be comfortable in the world. James had never been able to tell what she was thinking; the painter should not have been able to tell; he should have had to work his brush across a riddle.

When he went out the moon had only just appeared. It was huge and thick and darkly colored at his back, absorbent. He scarcely knew it was there, but he was screwed tight upon his thirst, and he walked again along the highway. He did not hear the crickets that had begun to crackle everywhere.

And later, later, on his way back, the moon was high and colorless, a perfect spot on the murky midnight. He stumbled in his joy and stupor, knowing not yet what he yearned for, knowing only that he was alive to the night and strangely exhilarated.

He saw the dead silver dog, stealthy in death, and he walked a wide way around it. He wanted to say serious things, but laughter grew up in him. His laughter rang out, rolled along the black bank of the creek below, the gray grass, the undulent way to the Wichitas. Oh, God, he thought, the clamorous night! He could hear everything distinctly now, the rasping of the crickets and the frogs, the wind turning, leaves sliding upon leaves, a motor in the far distance, the echo of his laughter dying away, and beyond that the laughter of God, God's laughter. It was all so beautiful to hear. And he opened his eyes wide and looked all around, and everything shone in his sight, and it was all so beautiful to see. He was involved in the light, enchanted. He said God, spoke the name of God, laughing with his teeth clenched, and he felt himself whirling in the light. The light was like frost on the hills; it lay out in the great round hollow of the plains, as far as he could see, shifting and quaking slowly, tumbling like a fog. Then the beauty was too much, and tears came to his eyes, and he kept saying the name God, God, God, until he choked on it. And through his tears he saw the moon, red and blue and green. A shaft of light like a bolt struck down in the meadow, not a stone's throw away, among chinaberry trees. There were deep colors in it, and it was brighter than the moon, and it took his breath away, and he wanted everyone to see it, especially the boy. Look, look, he thought, how God has drawn the sky with light. Light was laced among the willows; it set a brightness like fire upon the grass, and it rose and floated like smoke. It defined clouds in the sky, and it radiated from the clouds like fractures in glass, like spiderwebs. And suddenly he knew how small he was, how little he mattered in the laughter of God, not at all, really. He knew at once that this moment, the blink of an eye, held more beauty and wonder than he could know. He had not enough life to deal with it. He could only suffer the least part of it; he could only open his eyes and see what he could see of the world. And again he laughed together with God. And he thought: Wait a moment, God. Give me a moment. I have a moment, and it is too big for me, and I cannot hold it in my little hands. And you, God, you give me the night and the world. It is a good joke, and, God, we laugh. But I have seen how you draw the sky with light.

My parents about the time of their marriage.

THREE

1

THE SECOND WORLD WAR had nothing to do with my parents and me at first, certainly nothing of which I could be aware. But I see now that the war eventually determined our circumstances in numerous ways, and it became for me a kind of constant abstraction on the far edge of my mind. There came a time, indeed, when I could not have conceived of a world which was not somehow articulated in terms of "the war." For one thing there were markets, more or less directly related to "the war effort," of which we heard incessantly; jobs were everywhere, it seemed, and for my parents, who had begun their married life in hard times, there were opportunities. For another thing there was a kind of patriotic sympathy to those days, the romantic integrity of a cause, which was perceptible to me even then; I was becoming conscious of such things. And this, too, was a real spur to my imagination.

We moved to the Staked Plains (which country my Kiowa forebears knew well), where my father worked for an oil company as a draftsman. My mother found a job with the Civilian Personnel Office, then with the Office of the Provost Marshal, at the Hobbs Army Air Base.

Hobbs, New Mexico, was then a raw, undistinguished town on the flat, hot apron of the Staked Plains. It had not the color or the character of Gallup, although it had something of the same vigor and strength. New Mexican towns of the north are different one from another, or they are set in different landscapes; but in the south they seem all of a kind. Hobbs and Artesia and Carlsbad are thus related in their appearance and in their spirit, I believe, which is the hard spirit of the high, arboreal desert. And in this respect they are like the towns of west Texas: Lamesa, Midland, Plainview. There were many dusty dirt streets in Hobbs in my day, a good many wary old plainsmen and their sunbonneted wives, a "Niggertown," and a bakery that dispatched its breads in a horse-drawn wagon.

I see now that one experiences easily the ordinary things of life, the things which cast familiar shadows upon the sheer, transparent panels of time, and he perceives his experience in the only way he can, according to his age. There is a quality to the experience of any given place that is especially available to a child. I came to know Hobbs in a certain way, and in that way I knew it very well. I was in the third grade.

My best friend was Billy Don Johnson, a reddish, robust boy of great good humor and intense loyalty. He had a slight speech impediment, and he liked nothing better than to sing, for anyone who would hear him out, "Onward, Christian Soldiers," which he rendered with remarkable feeling. At such times he squeezed himself into a

84

terrible concentration, and his round red face bore the holy, irresistible aspect of an angel, a cherub gone slightly to seed. Even in the third grade his physique was impressive, thick and solid and low-slung. We all knew that his destiny lay in the middle of the line and a split second after the ball was snapped. I believe that he made All State in his senior year. The Hobbs Eagles are a traditional powerhouse in New Mexico high school football. We went religiously to their home games and were caught up in the frenzy of those brassy autumn nights. On the sidelines we expressed our pitiful adoration of our heroes, and we tackled each other viciously from behind.

It seems to me that half the boys of Hobbs were named Billy.

In the early forties Hobbs was fixed on the far fringe of the war, and yet there were moments of great immediacy, when it seemed to us that we were very close to the front. On Saturday afternoons at the Reel Theatre we cheered to those wonderful newsreels in which, out of nowhere, a Zero or an Me-109 suddenly swerved into our sights. It was the very maneuver, grand, irrevocable, fatal, we had been waiting for. The whole field of vision shuddered with our fire; the 50-caliber tracers curved out, fixing brilliant arcs upon the span, and struck; then there was a black burst of smoke, and the target went spinning down to death. Or, better, it simply disintegrated before our eyes, an instantaneous transformation of man and machine into thin air. Along with reading and writing we were taught to hate our enemies. Every day, after we had pledged allegiance to the flag, we sang—Billy Don louder than the rest—"Let's remember Pearl Harbor, as we do the Alamo," and I remember a picture postcard on which the cartoon faces of Hitler, Mussolini, and Tojo were represented on squares of toilet paper above the legend WIPE THEM OUT.

As a child, especially, my features belied the character of my ancient ethnic origin. (There are early photographs of me which might have been made thirty thousand years ago on the Bering Strait land bridge; just wide of the prehistoric camera's eye there stands a faithful dog of the chow strain, dragging a travois. My mother recalls that one day in Bayou le Batre, a pretty moppet was heard to say in my defense, "Well, I don't care if he *is* a Chinaman. *I* like him anyway." And as recently as my undergraduate days someone sitting next to me on the side of a swimming pool asked me from what part of Asia I had come. "Northern Mongolia," I replied.) In Hobbs, New Mexico, in 1943, I was suspected of that then dreadful association. Nearly every day on the playground someone would greet me with, "Hi'ya, Jap," and the fight was on. Now and then two or more patriots would gang up on me, and that's when Billy Don stepped in. As a team we compiled a formidable record.

I fell hopelessly in love with a girl named Kathleen. She had blond, curly hair and pale blue eyes that were wonderfully sad, and she wore ribbons and clean, crisp dresses. She kept to the company of other girls, and I followed her about at a discreet distance, wanting in some fresh stirring within me to snatch her up and carry her away to the mountains, wherever they were. What a pity, I now believe, that I did not at least tell her that she was pretty, though I suppose she knew. And when the stirring became a modest turbulence I fell in love again, with a dark, lithe girl whose name was Eugenia. She was several years my senior, and I went to school to her, as boys have gone to school to women always. She inspired dark rumors, for that was her calling, I believe. The older boys, whom my peers and I admired and emulated, spoke of her leeringly in terms that I could not yet fully understand, and so I adored her. I bought her a purse which cost three dollars, the whole of my Christmas allowance. That generosity, that extravagance which remains in some sense the ultimate in me, was lost upon her. She reacted not with gratitude— much less did she swoon—but with a kind of easy knowingness. And

in that affair I learned how to be a fool, a lesson that I have learned
again and again.

Billy Don was my true friend, and I was very much at home in his
house. His parents were wonderful, down-to-earth people, and they
were very good to me; it was in their nature, and they should not
have known how to be otherwise. Theirs was a large family, of which
Billy Don was the youngest, and there was a lot of activity in their
house. Mrs. Johnson was a large, jovial woman who cooked heroic
meals. On the nights that I spent there we woke up, Billy Don and I,
to the most wonderful smells, bacon and chops, breads and gravy,
coffee and cakes. Billy Don liked to sleep late, and it was difficult to
get him awake. I kneaded him, poked him in the ribs, pulled him
upright, and he sat interminably on the edge of the bed, dealing with
his shoes and socks. But after such a breakfast he ran on all day like a
clock. We prowled the streets of Hobbs, without which there was no
order in the universe, looking round all the corners for our destiny.

For a time Billy Don's father kept a little truck farm near the air
base, about eight miles from the town. Sometimes we went there to
chase the pigs about and to play at war out in that sweltering sand
country. We dug trenches and slithered like vipers through the brittle
brush, dragging our toy rifles across the minefields, hurling grenades
against the glassy dunes, the thousand bunkers that lay between us
and our glory, pausing only to treat our wounds and to grab at lizards
and horned toads or to drink Kool-Aid from our canteens. One day, in
July, when we were prisoners of war, we set out on a march from the
pigpen there, which was our concentration camp, towards the town.
We went on and on through infernal regions, through the morning
and afternoon. We went on until our heroism evaporated and the
game was given up and our mouths were full of cotton, and there was
nothing to do but go on. I believe that we walked fifteen miles in the
desert that day. We limped into Hobbs more dead than alive; Billy

Don dropped out at his house, and I went on to mine. When I arrived I spent the very last bit of my strength getting upon my bed. And even before my mother could place the cool, damp washcloth to my forehead I fell into the deepest sleep that I have ever known.

I was not much interested in the process of learning at school. I can only barely remember the sort of work that was put to us; it was a thing that was not congenial to my mind. The evil of recitation was real; I hated to be called upon. And even worse was the anticipation of it. I knew of no relief that was equal to that of the bell. My eyes were very weak, and I had about that time to wear eyeglasses. Eyeglasses conformed in no way at all to any notion that I had of myself, and I did away with them at every opportunity. Tommy, a shrimp of a boy, the menace of whose gaze was effectively exaggerated by means of round, thick, smudgy lenses, told on me consistently. I hoped that he would die.

My mother read to me, or she told me stories in which I had the leading part. And my father told me the old Kiowa tales. These were many times more exciting than anything I found at school; they, more than the grammars and arithmetics, nourished the life of my mind.

In my day there were two classifications of boys at Hobbs, the toughs and the sissies. I was big and strong, and so I most often aligned myself with the toughs. It was convenient to do so, for I had then a stake in the dominant society, and the world of children is simply informed by the principle of domination. On the other hand, some of the boys that I liked best were sissies, and I got on with them very well in the main. The truth is, I moved more easily across the dividing line, back and forth, than did most of my fellows, and I learned to deal in crude diplomacies, strategies of choice and adjustment.

The movies of those days were a great and dubious influence upon us; we were utterly seduced by them. On those Saturday afternoons at the Reel Theatre we were drawn into worlds of infinite possibility. Our taste ran to high adventure, and we cared much more for Sergeant York than for Mrs. Miniver, of course, but we devoured everything that came our way. It is strange how indelible are some of those impressions in my mind after many years—Lon Chaney, Jr., looking with both horror and infinite sadness at the full moon, for example. And for a boy bearing hard upon adolescence, how is it possible to forget Ingrid Bergman in *Casablanca*, say, or Hedy Lamarr in *White Cargo?* And we would not let go of the movies, but we lived in them for days afterwards. I remember that after we had seen *The Black Swan*, there were sword fights in the streets, and we battered each other mercilessly. Most of the swords were flimsy affairs, curtain weights and yardsticks; but mine was a length of doweling that I had pushed through a gelatin mold; it was a superior weapon, and with it I terrorized the neighborhood. Once, through a picket fence, I saw the Mummy moving across a moonlit yard, dragging his ancient foot. For good or bad, something of my belief was fashioned there, once and for all, among the shadows.

For a time my aunt Ethel and her son, John, lived at Hobbs and were our next-door neighbors. John was five years older than I, and I loved and admired him greatly. In the years of our association, which were largely confined to my childhood, he taught me many things by example, and he was always very tolerant of me, in spite of the difference in our ages. I must have been a bother to him on occasion, but he never let me know it. To the life between us I had little enough to contribute, but once, at Hobbs, I was given a chance to help him, and I did, and I have been grateful for that chance ever since. This is how it happened: I was coming home from school and I saw that there were eight or ten older boys on the lawn of the public library, John among them. He was standing apart from the others, and they were shouting at him. As I approached they surrounded him, and one of them hurled himself at John's back, grabbing him about the neck. John did not fall, but he threw the boy around and struck him in the face and the boy fell to the ground, his nose bleeding. I could not believe what was happening, and I was very much afraid and did not know what to do. And suddenly there was an awful quiet, a hard stillness, and I could feel the rage running there, and I wanted to run away; something was going to happen, something bad, in the next moment. Then John said softly, evenly, "Come here. Stand at my back, will you?—where I can't see." And I understood that he was talking to me, and I went to him and stood at his back, to see that no one jumped on him again. And then together we moved out of the circle and nothing happened and we got away. I never knew what the fight was about, but I never doubted that my cousin John was in the right.

I had about that time discovered the dark joy of masturbation. For a time the burden of guilt lay heavily on me, and I read in everyone's eyes that I had been found out, that I was perverted and depraved, though these large concepts were certainly crude and tentative in my mind. It was John who assuaged my guilt in this matter. He knew more than I did, but not so much more that he hadn't a genuine interest in my society, my education, and the salvation of my soul.

We gave each other model airplane kits for Christmas. My gift was so far inferior to John's that I was ashamed and cried. Not only did he give me the fine model airplane, but he assembled it for me as well.

2

It happened that we moved to a community called Los Llanos at the Hobbs Army Air Base and lived there for a year, but I continued in the same school, riding the bus each day. I was growing up. About that time my parents gave me a bicycle, and I rode everywhere on the base. I came to have a different sense of the war there. Hobbs was a B-17 base, and I formed a good impression of those "Flying Fortresses," which came in and went out incessantly. The war was being won from the bomb-bay doors of those planes; they were the workhorses of our air force, and they bore the brunt of the battle over Europe. They were superseded in the late stages of the war by the B-29s; it was a kind of upstaging that I have always resented a little. Some of those planes were badly damaged; they had acquired an awful character under fire, and they had flown home to die. I played in the catwalks of their carcasses—and my games were then a benediction— and extended their missions into the dreams of a child.

I try now to think of the war, of what it was to me as a child. It was almost nothing, and nothing of my innocence was lost in it. It was only later that I realized what had happened, what ancient histories had been made and remarked and set aside in a fraction of my lifetime, in an instant. And *there* is the loss of innocence, in retrospection, in the safe distance of time. There are the clocks of shame; we tell the lie of time, and our hearts are broken.

3

Children trust in language. They are open to the power and beauty of language, and here they differ from their elders, most of whom have come to imagine that they have found words out, and so much of magic is lost upon them. Creation says to the child: Believe in this tree, for it has a name.

If you say to a child, "The day is almost gone," he will take you at your word and will find much wonder in it. But if you say this to a man whom the world has disappointed, he will be bound to doubt it. *Almost* will have no precision for him, and he will mistake your meaning. I can remember that someone held out his hand to me, and in it was a bird, its body broken. *It is almost dead.* I was overcome with the mystery of it, that the dying bird should exist entirely in its dying. J. V. Cunningham has a poem, "On the Calculus":

> From almost nought to almost all I flee,
> And *almost* has almost confounded me;
> Zero my limit, and infinity.

I can almost see into the summer of a year in my childhood. I am again in my grandmother's house, where I have come to stay for a month or six weeks—or for a time that bears no common shape in my mind, neither linear nor round, but it is a deep dimension, and I am lonely in it. Earlier in the day—or in the day before, or in another day—my mother and father have driven off. Somewhere on a road, in Texas, perhaps, they are moving away from me, or they are settled in a room away, away, thinking of me or not, my father scratching his head, my mother smoking a cigarette and holding a little dog in her lap. There is a silence between them and between them and me. I am thoughtful. I see into the green, transparent base of a kerosene lamp; there is a still circle within it, the surface of a deeper transparency. Do I bring my hands to my face? Do I turn or nod my head? Something of me has just now moved upon the metal throat of the lamp, some distortion of myself, nonetheless recognizable, and I am distracted. I look for my image then in the globe, rising a little in my chair, but I see nothing but my ghost, another transparency, glass upon glass, the wall beyond, another distortion. I take up a pencil and set the point against a sheet of paper and define the head of a boy, bowed slightly, facing right. I fill in quickly only a few details, the line of the eye, the curve of the mouth, the ear, the hair—all in a few simple strokes. Yet there is life and expression in the face, a conjugation that I could not have imagined in these markings. The boy looks down at something that I cannot see, something that lies apart from the picture plane. It might be an animal, or a leaf, or the drawing of a boy. He is thoughtful and well-disposed. It seems to me that he will smile in a moment, but there is no laughter in him. He is contained in his expression—and fixed, as if the foundation upon which his flesh and bones are set cannot be shaken. I like him certainly, but I don't know who or where or what he is, except that he is the inscrutable reflection of my own vague certainty. And then I write, in my child's hand, beneath the drawing, "This is someone. Maybe this is Mammedaty. This is Mammedaty when he was a boy." And I wonder at the words. *What are they?* They stand, they lean and run upon the page of a manuscript—I have made a manuscript, rude and illustrious. The page bears the likeness of a boy—so simply crude the likeness to some pallid shadow on my blood—and his name consists in the letters there, the words, the other likeness, the little, jumbled drawings of a ritual, the nominal ceremony in which all homage is returned, the legend of the boy's having been, of his going on. I have said it; I have set it down. I trace the words; I touch myself to the words, and they stand for me. My mind lives among them, moving ever, ever going on. I lay the page aside, I imagine. I pass through the rooms of the house, slowly, pausing at familiar objects: a quiver of arrows on the wall, old photographs in oval frames, beaded emblems, a Bible, an iron bedstead, a calendar for the year 1942. Mammedaty lies ten years in the ground at Rainy Mountain Cemetery. What is there, *just there*, in the earth, in the bronze casket, under Keahdinekeah's shawl? I go out into the yard; the shadows are long to the east, and the sunlight has deepened and the red earth is darkened now to umber and the grasses are burnished. Across the road, where the plain is long and undulant and bears the soft sheen of rose gentian and rose mallow, there are figures like fossils in the prisms of the air. I see a boy standing still in the distance, only his head and shoulders visible above the long, luminous grass, and from the place where he stands there comes the clear call of a meadowlark. It is so clear, so definite in the great plain! I believe that it circles out and out, that it touches like ancient light upon the thistles at Saddle Mountain, upon the broken floor of Boke's store, upon the thin shadows that follow on the current of the Washita. And round on the eastern shelves I see the crooked ravines which succeed to the sky, a whirlwind tracing a red, slanting line across the middle distance, and there in the roiling dust a knoll, a gourd dance and give-away, and Mammedaty moves among the people, answers to his name; low thunder rolls upon the drum. A boy leads a horse into the circle, the horse whipping its haunches around, rattling its blue hooves on the hard earth, rolling its eyes and blowing. There are eagle feathers fixed with ribbons in the braided mane, a bright red blanket on the back of the black, beautiful hunting horse. The boy's arms are taut with the living weight, the wild will and resistance of the horse, swinging the horse round in a tight circle, to the center of the circle where Mammedaty stands waiting to take the reins and walk, with dignity, with the whole life of the hunting horse, away. It is good and honorable to be made such a gift—the gift of this horse, this hunting horse—and honorable to be the boy, the intermediary in whose hands the gift is passed. My fingers are crisped, my fingertips bear hard

My grandfather Mammedaty.

upon the life of this black horse. *Oh my grandfather, take hold of this horse. It is good that you should be given this horse to hold in your hands, that you should lead it away from this holy circle, that such a thing should happen in your name.* And the southern moon descends; light like phosphorus appears in the earth, blue and bone, clusters of blue-black bunch grass, pocks in pewter. Flames gutter momently in the arbor and settle to the saffron lamps; fireflies flicker on the lawn; frogs begin to tell of the night; and crickets tell of the night, but there is neither beginning nor end in their telling. The old people arrive, the thin-limbed, deep-eyed men in their hats and braids, the round-faced women in their wide half sleeves and fringed shawls, apron-bound, carrying pots and pans and baskets of food—fried bread, boiled cracked corn, melons, pies and cakes—and for hours my grandmother has been cooking meat, boiled beef, fried chicken, chicken-fried beefsteaks, white and brown gravies. *Cohn' Tsotohah, Tsoai-talee, come here; I want to tell you something.* I sit at an old man's knee. I don't know who he is, and I am shy and uncomfortable at first; but there is delight in his eyes, and I see that he loves me. There are many people in the arbor; everyone listens. *Cohn', do you see the moon?* The full, white moon has receded into the southeast; it is a speckled moon; through the arbor screen it shimmers in the far reaches of the night. *Well, do you see?—there is a man in the moon. This is how it happened: Saynday was hungry. Oh, everyone was hungry then; the buffalo were keeping away, you know. Then Saynday's wife said to him, "Saynday, tomorrow the men are going on a hunt. You must go with them and bring back buffalo meat." "Well, yes," said Saynday. And the next day he went out on the hunt. Everyone found buffalo, except Saynday. Saynday could find no buffalo, and so he brought some tomatoes home to his wife. She was angry, but she said to him, "Saynday, tomorrow the men are going hunting again. Now I tell you that you must go with them, and you must bring back buffalo meat." "Well, yes," said Saynday. And again he went on the hunt. Everyone found buffalo, except Saynday. He could find no*

96

buffalo, and so he brought tomatoes home to his wife again. She was very angry, but she said to him, "Saynday, tomorrow the men are going hunting again. You must go with them, and you must bring back buffalo meat." "Well, yes," said Saynday. And Saynday went out on the hunt for the third time. And it was just the same: everyone found Buffalo, except Saynday. Saynday could find no buffalo, and so he brought tomatoes home to his wife again. She was so angry that she began to beat him with a broom. Saynday ran, but she ran after him, beating him with the broom. He ran faster and faster, until he got away, and then he wanted to hide. He hid in the moon. There he is now in the moon, and he will not come down because he is afraid of his wife. My people laugh with me; I am created in the old man's story, in his delight. There is a black bank and lightning in the north, the moon higher and holding off, the Big Dipper on a nail at the center of the sky. I lie down on the wide bench at my grandmother's back. The prayer meeting goes on, the singing of Christian hymns in Kiowa, now and then a gourd dance song.

There would be old men and old women in my life.

I invented history. In April's thin white light, in the white landscape of the Staked Plains, I looked for tracks among the tufts of coarse, brittle grass, amid the stones, beside the tangle of dusty hedges. When I look back upon those days—days of infinite promise and steady adventure and the certain sanctity of childhood—I see how much was there in the balance. The past and the future were simply the large contingencies of a given moment; they bore upon the present and gave it shape. One does not pass through time, but time enters upon him, in his place. As a child, I knew this surely, as a matter of fact; I am not wise to doubt it now. Notions of the past and future are essentially notions of the present. In the same way an idea of one's ancestry and posterity is really an idea of the self. About this time I was formulating an idea of myself.

97

Miss Johnson said Mayre not Mary why doesn't she talk the way she's supposed to and that Tommy the dirty rat I'll knock his block off and not care if he tells he tells everything and the time Billy Don and I got spanked because we were throwing snowballs and broke a window the one on the side not the driver's side and the lady was smiling until that happened driving slowly and smiling and the glass went crack it was only cracked and then she got mad not really mad but oh oh now we have to do something about that this and that you'll never know just how much I love you I didn't want to go to Mrs. Powell's because she has all those nice things in her house and you have to sit still and she watches you and one time she wouldn't even let me eat an orange in her car it smells she said and your fingers get sticky she said and I don't like her crummy cactus garden either well I like it but there are a lot of better cactuses over by Billy Don's dad's place I wonder who that girl was the soldier's girl on the library lawn and they were having their picture taken and the soldier was trying to touch her down there and she was giggling and I heard the twins laughing about it and I wanted to laugh too but the girl was pretty and I thought she should not have let him do that she's really good and decent probably maybe she was ashamed and didn't know what to do but laugh that's the way I am sometimes oh my gosh mom and dad heard me yesterday and I was singing You're in the army now you're not behind the plow you'll never get rich you son of a bitch and they heard me and weren't mad but said not to sing that even if all the other kids were singing it I think dad wasn't sure and said he said son of a bee didn't he and mom said yes he did and I did but I didn't know it I really didn't know it and one time in the arbor Lucius told me I said some bad words and Aunt Clara heard me and I didn't know I had said them how could I just forget like that Lucius and Marland and Justin Lee and Ponzi we used to play around the arbor and the outhouse and tell jokes and smoke why did Burt tell me he was smoking oak leaves and that was all right well he's a lot older but I bet that wasn't oak leaves maybe it was anyway John was in the

shower and I was playing at the sink in the kitchen and I wasn't
trying to make the water hot but he thought I was well what's today
Wednesday or Thursday no Saturday Saturday at the show when the
crook came out on the porch and he started to smoke a cigarette and
everyone thought Bob had got killed I didn't though the crook fell
then and we all yelled like crazy next time old Bob will get in trouble
again and Hopalong Cassidy is coming to the Reel Fred Jackson is a
sergeant is he yes but he got busted someone said for fighting for
hitting his commanding officer he's pretty okay to me why does he
like those records Glenn Miller and Tommy Dorsey and Harry James
Sleepy lagoon mom and dad too dad likes that music I think maybe
at the Avalon When the lights go on again all over the world oh Billy
Don and Burleigh those dumb guys this morning no yesterday no this
morning I had to keep them quiet because mom was sleeping she
loves to sleep late I don't like it though I like to get up but I had
breakfast in bed I made it eggs and toast and jam and I took it to my
bed and ate it in bed well I don't do it all the time I pledge
allegiance to the flag indivisible My country 'tis of thee sweet land of
liberty oh gosh Guadalcanal it isn't so bad to get shot I guess if it's a
flesh wound get the medic but they strafe the beach John says the
Zeros are more maneuverable but a lot slower than the P-39s and the
Mustangs what do they call the P-38s they're so awful fast I'm in a
Bell P-39 okay no a Flying Tiger okay sons of the rising sun this is for
my kid brother ha gotcha oh oh there's a Zero on my tail
eeeeeeooooooooooow lost him in the clouds just dropped down and let
him go over me and climbed up oh he can't believe it he's in my
sights crosshairs there Tojo that's for the Sullivans well Chuck you
can paint four more Zeros on old Sally here no I'm okay thanks
honorable colonel we must stop Momaday he comes from nowhere
from the sun I tell you he's not human they say he's an Indian that
he wears an eagle feather has the eyes the heart of an eagle he must
be stopped there son of the rising sun that's for Major Anderson
eeeeeeeeeeooooooooow what oh another medal oh it was nothing sir it

was for my kid brother sir he got his over Burma it was for the Sullivan boys and Major Anderson what lead the eagle squadron yessir thank you sir it's a great honor

I don't want to see Louise again not since I made that lemonade and she was the only one who bought some shoot for a nickel it was and she came across the street and said it was good and cold and thanked me I hate Henry Aldridge too what was that really neat program The Monkey's Paw The Most Dangerous Game The Mollé Mystery Theatre

I asked Billy Don if his mom and dad told him stories when he went to bed and he laughed once upon a time there were three pigs Rootie and Tootie and Pootie and Mickey Mouse and Minnie Mouse Scotty had a brand-new red car and it was snowing outside Billy Don began to laugh he got so tickled and we were all surprised because gosh it was right there in school what is it Billy Don the teacher said and he said oh nothing you wouldn't understand I was just thinking and we all laughed like heck it was so funny Ida was sent out of the room and I felt funny about that that she was sent outside and knew that we were all talking about her gee and Miss Marshall said you must not be cruel some people do not have as much as you do and Ida can't help it her clothes are old and dirty I found her crying in the bathroom and you must not be cruel you must make her feel that you are all her friends and then we all went out of our way to be friendly even Charles you're an Indian Charles said and I said yes Indians are no good he said and I said you're a liar he can't stand to be called that gosh anything but that and he's so tough so I took it back

Grandma I miss you I feel sorry for you when I come to see you and see you and go away I know you're lonely I like to see you I love to see you in the arbor cooking and talking to us you goot boy you say Scotty you goot boy and you used to carry me on your back in your shawl and hold me in your lap and I came to sleep with you and you're so soft and warm and I like the smell of you your hair is so

thick and heavy it is so black except for the gray here and there you
buy me candy corn and candy orange slices jellybeans animal crackers
I like to watch you sew and make beadwork let's go to town grandma
to the store you have so much money always Uncle Jimmy has money
sometimes he buys me something down by Lonewolf his land
everyone says he's going to give me some land someday oh yes Miss
Marshall my dad's people the Kiowas they have a lot of land in
Oklahoma my uncle is going to give me some land quite a lot of it
someday no ma'am he's not a farmer but he owns farmland yes
ma'am it's very strange well yes ma'am I'm a Kiowa yes ma'am I'm
sure it's not Keeowa no ma'am I can't say the Lord's Prayer in Kiowa
I can't say much of anything really my dad can yes ma'am I *am*
proud to be so American I know it ma'am Lay that pistol down babe

Oh I feel so dumb I can't answer all those questions I don't know
how to be a Kiowa Indian my grandmother lives in a house it's like
your house Miss Marshall or Billy Don's house only it doesn't have
lights and light switches and the toilet is outside and you have to
carry wood in from the woodpile and water from the well but that
isn't what makes it Indian its my grandma the way she is the way she
looks her hair in braids the clothes somehow yes the way she talks she
doesn't speak English so well Scotty you goot boy she says wait I
know why it's an Indian house because there are pictures of Indians
on the walls photographs of people with long braids and buckskin
clothes dresses and shirts and moccasins and necklaces and beadwork
yes that's it and there is Indian stuff all around blankets and shawls
bows and arrows everyone there acts like an Indian everyone even me
and my dad when we're there we eat meat and everyone talks Kiowa
and the old people wear Indian clothes well those dresses dark blue
and braids and hats and there is laughing Indians laugh a lot and they
sing oh yes they love to sing sometimes when an old man comes to
visit he sits in the living room and pretty soon he just begins to sing
loud with his eyes closed but really loud and his head nodding and in
the arbor there are sometimes pretty often a lot of people and lots to

eat and everyone sings and sometimes there are drums too and it goes on through the night *that's* Indian my dad sets out poles on the river and we eat catfish *that's* Indian and grandma goes to Rainy Mountain Baptist Church *that's* Indian and my granddad Mammedaty is buried at Rainy Mountain and some of the stones there have peyote pictures on them and you can hear bobwhites there and see terrapins and scissortails and that's Indian too

I gave mom Evening in Paris perfume and a little handkerchief and she was thrilled said so Mother's Day but when I was just a kid last year two years ago I can't remember I went on an Easter egg hunt at school no the park and I got some Easter eggs but I ate them and brought home nothing and was ashamed forever

I'll have a sweetheart in the war and she will look like Faye Emerson when I was at grandma's I had a picture of Faye Emerson it was in a magazine I think and she was my sweetheart and I talked to her all the time I love you darling don't worry oh I know it's tough war is heck but though there's one motor gone we will still carry on Faye yes Faye Emerson Montclair New Jersey if anything happens to me Billy Don see that she gets this letter we were going to be married and live in a little bungalow out west hear that Billy Don that's it time to go thumbs up buddy old pal take care of things take care of that leg pal I'll miss you Oh don't sit under the apple tree with anyone else but me anyone else but me anyone else but me I'm gonna dance with the dolly with the hole in her stocking while her knees keep a knocking while her toes keep a rocking hi'ya Hitler here's one for Major Jordan okay Billy Don you take the ball see and lateral to me and then run out straight sure I can throw it that far can you run that far they won't know what hit them there's a game tonight isn't there oh I love the games the air is cold and full of music and shouting the field is so green under the lights and the stripes are so white so much excitement I heard one of the high-schoolers say the Cavemen were going to win that if they couldn't win on the field they were sure as heck going to beat them off the field everything depends on the game this game the Eagles and the Cavemen I got as close as I could I could see how hard they were playing playing so hard they were crying some of them their arms and legs bandaged and blood showing through cussing at each other I was kind of scared and the quarterback called the signals and the ball was in the air and the helmets and pads cracked together oh it was grand I love football nothing could be better than to be a great football player a back a quarterback or a fullback I told the Canons that I was a tailback but I don't know what that is

Maybe I'll go to Kirby's house but I don't like him well he's all right but he's funny his folks are funny like that time I knocked on the door and no one answered and in the yard I picked up a piece of wood black wood a little block nailed to a big block and I was looking at it it looked like a German submarine and Kirby yelled out the window and everyone was there inside and told me to put it down it was his or what was I doing with it anyway but I wasn't going to take it steal it but it felt just like I was stealing it the way they spied on me I didn't know what to do but they were watching me all the time hiding there in the house why don't they answer the door Kirby's dad was in the army a long time ago the First World War and he was gassed Kirby said and there was a gas mask in the closet there I had never seen one a real one before and Kirby and I when we were little used to play war and our rations were always mustard sandwiches I don't know why but they were always mustard sandwiches the bread got dry and the mustard too and darker funny color like sometimes the sand like the canyons at Chinle yeah it's Begay sir he comes from Chinle Arizona I knew him yessir eeeeeeeooooooow puh uh uh uh uh uh uh there you son of the rising sun that's for Corporal Begay the nurse sir oh her name is Faye yessir her father is Doctor Emerson of Montclair New Jersey very rich oh that time at Chinle Jimmy King mom said Jimmy King dressed up like Santa Claus and woke me up I was so excited scared I guess I didn't know what to do I couldn't say anything I just sat up in bed and my eyes were big mom said Jimmy

103

was a boxer mom said a terrific boxer dad said Golden Gloves and he could beat guys twice his size or was it Shiprock Jimmy King came from Shiprock there was Sylvia oh gosh I was little then just a kid but I remember Sylvia's birthday party and I took a crummy present a coloring book maybe was it raining it was dark then Faye came over and we did that thing on the bed standing up she asked me if I knew how sure I said Ponzi and Justin Lee told me mom came in and said what are you doing and Faye told her said that word and mom told me not to do it again she told me later when everyone had gone but dad was there and he said what what did he do and never mind mom said gosh I was just a kid then Onward Christian soldiers the Canons kidnapped Chiquita and left a note for mom pay fifty dollars or you'll never see this dog again earlier I was throwing Chiquita up in the air letting her fall on the bed she didn't like it but I did dad teases her and she gets mad and growls and snaps at him she's so smart mom says and she doesn't like anyone the way she likes mom and those dogs Billy Don's dogs got married and we watched and Billy Don got really scared and went yelling they're stuck they're stuck and JJ turned the hose on them

That really old woman across the creek what's her name Keahdinekeah the way she looks gray hair so thin wrinkled skin scary eyes gray eyes and can't see the way she smells and she cries she reaches out and her hands are so little and soft and her voice is so high and crying like a baby's voice eh neh neh neh neh then she cries yes that's Indian dad says his dad used to take him in a wagon to Anadarko and they would stop eat watermelons in the shade that's Indian my dad's a great artist he's painting that picture of a war dancer maybe a buffalo hunt and somebody's going to win it at school or the PTA I don't know only I said he would do it so he has to do it dad says grandma's getting old and she likes for all of us to come home and she hugs me and says eh neh neh neh neh Scotty you goot boy and sometimes I sleep in the arbor it's cool out there and Jimmy and Ralph sleep out there the benches are hard but grandma puts lots

104

of covers on the benches and the covers are cool and the moonlight comes in but grandma has prayer meetings in the arbor and they go on and I get so sleepy but first it's fun because there are kids there and the kids don't want to stay in the arbor and sing and talk we run around outside oh but when aunt Clara and uncle Dick and Marland and Lucius are there it's good it's fun they always bring lots of food candy and cookies Kool-Aid toys too surprises I love to go to get the ice it's so cold in the icehouse it feels so good because it's so hot outside and I get so thirsty we get a big block of ice fifty pounds I guess and take it home to the icebox in the arbor and then ice in everything tea and soda pop and we can have ice cream and the icebox is full all the time she cooks all the time and the wind blows there are berries down there pecans by the river so dark there

Maybe I will see Mammedaty he will be there just appear not in a dream but really a vision like mom's mother the way she came beside the bed and she was an angel and was just there who are you maybe I will say but I will know who it is maybe he will look like that picture in the same clothes holding the feathers not smiling but looking just so calm hello are you in heaven grandpa yes I am in heaven well how is it there it is all right but it isn't what everyone says it is what everyone thinks is it beautiful grandpa no not beautiful but it is very quiet very still are there others there grandpa are your mom and dad there no those old people they did not come here but it is all right can you leave yes sometimes if someone wants you needs you I need you don't I grandpa well yes and I wanted to talk to you it is good that we talk together how many Indians are in heaven grandpa I don't know oh grandpa I love you I want you to tell me stories the stories you used to tell my dad I told him many stories he will tell you will he tell me everything no not everything not even all he knows but it is all right it is all right will you tell me about your grandmother the one who was captured is she there no she is not here I have not seen her is Jesus there grandpa I have not seen him but I believe that he is here will I go to heaven grandpa I don't know

105

but it is all right you must not be afraid were you afraid to die no because I saw many things and you will see many things are you going will you come again no I will not come again but if I need you if you need me

Well I have a granddad Theodore Scott his big dog Chief horse Prince once he had a mule and I rode that mule through the barn door but there wasn't room to go through not enough room to go through that door I don't know how we got inside I told everyone mom and dad and granddad and no one could understand how it happened I could have been killed I guess when I get a horse he will have eyes like Prince beautiful eyes granddad was a sheriff too and he shot someone I think and a lot of people tried to shoot him he was too good for them he wasn't afraid mom says he's not afraid but he sleeps with a gun under his pillow Burleigh doesn't believe it so don't I don't care it's true I've seen the gun there I have seen it dad says not to be afraid I don't think that guy will take my football again he grabbed my football I was walking through the yard the high school yard and he grabbed my football and knocked my ice cream down it fell in the dirt and he threw the football to another guy and they played with it keep away and I couldn't get it back didn't know what to do finally they got tired I guess and gave it to me but I was so late dad and I went to the high school to the principal's office and they brought that big guy in and he said he wasn't afraid of my dad but of course he was and I guess he was mad because I told on him and I hope I don't see him anymore and I hope Kathleen didn't see me when they took my ball well girls don't understand they just don't understand like that time at Louise's house when we were playing games and then we sang and I kept turning around to see that pretty big girl older and really pretty and I just wanted to look at her only pretty soon she started crying and everyone wanted to know what was wrong and Mr. Roth tried to make her stop crying calm her down and said Marie what's wrong and she was crying and said oh they all look at me like I had horns and it was me all my fault and I thought

106

My grandfather Theodore Scott. Fort Sam Houston.

I had done something bad terrible but it was just a misunderstanding I thought she was really pretty that's all

And that pretty girl next door Priscilla she's so dumb and Alvin her brother he's so dumb all he does is talk about God and the Bible and church and that time he kept asking me about prayers my prayers and I said he descended into hell and on the third day he arose again from the dead and he ascended into heaven and Alvin said what you mean Jesus went to hell and I didn't know so I said yeah I guess so and he told his sister and his mom and dad and I wanted him to shut up but he told everybody that I said Jesus went to hell and I didn't know what to do that time either

Well I might go to West Point I told mom that I was probably going to West Point and she said well we'll see you can probably go to West Point if you really want to I want to but maybe my eyes aren't good enough Tommy said you have to have really good eyes my eyes are pretty bad I guess the doctor said I would have to wear glasses how long I asked him and he said well you'll probably have to wear them all your life the Indians didn't wear glasses not the Kiowas how can you hunt buffalo with glasses on I broke my glasses where is West Point anyway They died with their boots on Custer was at West Point and he liked onions Taking a chance on love

Miss Johnson said Mayre not Mary and she says mary not merry mary Christmas Christmas I got boxing gloves and a football and a really good pen once I got a train I got boxing gloves real ones then everybody wanted to box with my gloves we had a tournament and I knocked Earl out well he didn't fall down but he acted really funny knocked out I hit him pretty hard I guess the twins are always fighting each other and they both have a lot of scars they're tough and they get in a lot of trouble after school last week they got in a big fight and Seldon was on top of Meldon hitting him hard in the face Meldon was crying but he was talking really dirty calling Seldon terrible names and blood was all over the place and we were all watching it was so terrible and Seldon better kill Meldon while he's

on top and then a lady drove by and stopped and she was really upset
and she bawled us all out and said she was going straight to the
principal and Norman said aw ma'am they're brothers Billy Don told
me the twins used to hit each other over the head with milk bottles
the Mollé Mystery Theatre Amos 'n' Andy how *do* you do Mom said
she heard me telling those guys Billy Don and Burleigh to be quiet
mom's sleeping and that was sweet she said she really thought that
was great of me and dad's always saying that's great sometimes he
goes to Midland or Odessa I wish I could go we used to go out in a
pickup at Chinle with Blackie in the back and the Navajo kids would
see us and Blackie barked like crazy oh but that time at San Carlos
when that crazy guy on the white horse chased me and mom and
mom was scared and I guess I was really scared too but I can't
remember so well but mom talks about it a lot and dad wasn't there
and the guy was drunk and crazy and really mean and we ran to the
trading post and it was closed and mom pounded on the door and
finally the trader opened up and let us in and said it was a good thing
he was there oh those Apaches they have beautiful horses one day I
went to Mr. Patayama's house there and he was taking a nap and
Mrs. Patayama told me to be quiet and mom was mad at me because
I had bothered those dumb people I was in a program at the school
there and I said I only regret that I have but one life to give for my
country Nathan Hale Joe Louis beat Buddy Baer in the first round A
Tree Grows in Brooklyn

My name that's Indian my names Tsotohah Tsoai-talee Kiowa
George gave me that name Kiowa George Poolaw on his gravestone at
Rainy Mountain Pohd-lohk those funny names Pohd-lohk Kau-au-ointy
that's Indian Mammedaty Huan-toa and mom Natachee too that's
Indian the round dance holding hands moving round sideways singing
the dresses swaying those beautiful shawls and moccasins beadwork
the war dancers feather bustles bells quills we went somewhere
Carnegie or Anadarko or Hobart that time there was a dance and
give-away oh it was fine all the colors everyone was wearing such fine

clothes the dancers had fans and rattles there was one big drum those
men four or five were beating that drum like making thunder the
ground seemed to shake and the dancers their feet seemed to make
the thunder how do they do it keep time that way so perfectly that's
Indian and when they stopped the give-away those women put lots of
things down on the ground heck anybody could just go out there and
take them blankets and stuff money too but sometimes they call out
the names Indian names and those people come out and get gifts dad
got a blanket Pendleton blanket plaid red and blue and green mom
got a shawl black with red flowers that old man gave me some money
two dollars two dollar bills they were new they were folded once the
long way like paper airplanes and Jimmy and Lester gave me money
too they always give me money that's Indian that give-away it's funny
it takes such a long time you get bored well I get bored if you don't
get anything and have to watch just sit there talking maybe resting
and the boy the water boy comes around with a bucket of water and
a dipper and the dancers drink it's so hot and all the names are called
out Goombi Poolaw Tsoodle Tonamah Poorbuffalo Whitehorse those
funny names Marland told me someone's name was Chester Meat
and he got so tickled it was somehow it was really funny like Billy
Don that time and we all laughed Chester Meat and we all really
laughed that's Indian Chester Meat you'd be so nice to come home
to dad said one time Mammedaty got a horse at the give-away a black
horse really a good one well I guess it was the best horse in the world
it was black dad said and it had a red blanket on its back and it
pranced and danced around and there were feathers in its hair its
mane and tail and that time too a girl dad said a beautiful girl in a
buckskin dress beautiful beadwork white buckskin she had hair so
black and black eyes dad said she was given a name at the give-away
and it was good dad said a good thing to be given a name there and
the girl was very beautiful and everyone was honored everyone
honored her because of that maybe I would have married her if I had
been there did she look like Faye Emerson no Minnehaha that's

110

Indian hey when was that I was in Roswell I went to a show it was a
good show all about was it Billy the Kid there was a Mexican his
name was Jose I hadn't heard that name Jose before and it sounded
good to me and I kept saying it over and over again Jose Jose Jose
Jose Jose I liked it and mom said she visited Mrs. Garrett Elizabeth
I think and her dad Mrs. Garrett's dad killed Billy the Kid well yes I
killed the little varmint of course yes he came in you see the room
was dark very dark you couldn't see really but he said who is it or
who's here or there or something like that I squeezed the trigger
there was a flash in the room I saw him he fell oh yeah well listen
here Garrett go for your gun Garrett gun Garrett gun Garrett I'll give
you the chance you never gave poor Billy Garrett go for it what
you're not afraid are you Garrett oh call me Jose just say that I'm a
friend of the man you shot down in cold blood *pough* that's for Billy
pough that's for Billy's girl Faye *pough* that's for Billy's mom that
gray-haired little woman back in Silver City *pough* that's for Billy and
me Billy and me we rode the range together

All right Angelo look we can do it we're only behind by six points I
can get clear look I know I can get clear look just watch me I'll go
right down the sideline get the ball to me okay on three oh yes I've
got it here they come I stiff-arm one get the knees high high pour it
on now you're fast fast ladies and gentlemen this is incredible it
looked like a run all the way but Bertelli hid the ball and at the last
moment flipped a pass to Momaday in the flat and now the chief has
it on his own thirty-five he stiff-arms one man slides off another my
lord how did he get out of that there were four blue jerseys he was
completely boxed in five six seven men had a shot at him oh now he's
reversing his field the stands are going wild two more tacklers get
their hands on him but he gets away simply incredible I don't believe
my eyes he's at the fifty the forty-five the forty the thirty-five only
one man now between him and the goal the thirty the twenty-five he
feints he spins he side-steps the lone defender is helpless ladies and
gentlemen tied in a knot Momaday trots now walks the ball across the

goal line touchdown Notre Dame ladies and gentlemen that play covered ninety-seven yards from scrimmage the fans are wild the most brilliant bit of broken-field running this announcer has ever seen

The dog Wahnookie at Shiprock German shepherd would not let anyone come near me stood between me and anyone else anyone she didn't know well I was just a baby then learning to walk I guess once I went to sleep outside under the slide in the playground and dad came looking for me with a switch and I was afraid but I said hi dad and before he could get mad he said hi and everything was all right oh that geography Sacramento is the capital of California Olympia is the capital of Washington Pierre is the capital of South Dakota is it I think so Albany is the capital of New York arithmetic I hate it what I do sometimes is draw in the books move the pencil down through the words not through the words but around the words well among the words not touching them oh make believe I'm running with the football the words are tacklers move the pencil real fast if you touch a word you're tackled I showed Billy Don now he does it too maybe I'll spend the night at Billy Don's house but last time I got homesick in the night and went home and mom was up sitting at her dresser and she was glad to see me and missed me too and did we whip cream stiff with sugar JJ sings those dirty songs but they are funny tells jokes daddy what's that that's my roll of bills mama what's that that's my purse daddy will you put your roll of bills in mama's purse and the girls of France

Last summer I had that little dagger that Mexican dagger from Mrs. Ball's shop I think and I practiced and practiced throwing it holding the point very lightly between my finger and thumb how was it the dagger felt just right balanced just easily there and finally I could stick it in the ground almost every time then there was the horny toad on the ground and I just saw it and just automatically I flipped the dagger down and it went right through the horny toad I didn't mean to do it it just happened gosh the horny toad wasn't dead but it had the dagger sticking through it and it seemed just the same looking around and I had to get my dagger back but I didn't like to touch it then but I did and I threw the horny toad off and it didn't die or act hurt even but I was a little bit sick I think then afterwards I thought it was pretty neat and I told Billy Don and all the kids you don't want to make any sudden moves when I've got that Mexican dagger it just flicks out like the tongue of a snake partner oh yes like the time this dumb kid jumped on me from behind we were on the playground at lunchtime or recess and this dumb kid jumped on my back and I threw him over my shoulder and he fell on his head and started to cry and I was scared he was hurt and I wanted to say I'm sorry but there were these girls watching and one of them said gee he must be tough and I really liked that so I didn't apologize heck it wasn't my fault the dumb jerk that will teach him to sneak attack it was just a reflex action like throwing the Mexican dagger and that time I threw Leroy Woodley into the lockers it wasn't all that hard but it made a terrific bang like a bomb or something and it scared everybody me too but he wasn't hurt I am tough I guess really tough but Billy Don is tougher

Oh I have had a toothache don't tell me about toothaches there's nothing worse I had a bad toothache I was lying on the divan crying and mom and dad were trying to make me feel better but I just kept crying softly I think bravely and dad asked me what would make me feel better an official Boy Scout hatchet I said and he said okay I could have it

Last night driving along the sky was so red and streaked and everything so still the ground big and black my dad singing Indian songs my mom talking to him and laughing talking to me and laughing and Chiquita on her lap and the flare out there in the fields the smell of the place but going on driving on out and away from Hobbs towards Jal Caprock the ground so big and black the air so cool after the hot hot afternoon the sound of the wind rushing by star star shining bright first star I've seen tonight I wish I may I wish I might have the wish I wish tonight oh please I wish

Miss Johnson said Mayre not Mary and if Jeanine doesn't come to school on Monday I'll put one of those rubber mice or snakes in her desk the sky so red really red and beautiful it was then it was dark all around the headlights jumping around and I put my hand out the window and felt the wind so cool so hard on my hand I guess we were going fast and other stars were around all around there were so many and so close sometimes you see shooting stars the stars were so close last night when we got so far from town that there was no light on the sky no light but the stars on the sky and we stopped dad stopped the car and mom and dad and I and Chiquita got out and looked at the stars there were so many you couldn't begin to count them and some of them were so close together they were like water on a window when you move rain around on the window with your hand I wanted to rub my hand across the sky to see the stars move and run and spread out on the sky the sky was so black so purple but there were so many stars and the stars were so bright the black was closed out almost there was the sky full of stars and made you shiver to see them to feel the cold to hear that the stars were so quiet

4

But I was yet a child, and I lay low at Hobbs, feeling for the years in which I should find my whole self. And I had the strong, deceptive patience of a child, had not to learn it as patience but only to persist in it. Patience is what children have; it is especially theirs to have. I grew tall, and I entered into the seventh grade. I sat looking into books; there were birds on the lawn, chirping. Girls ambled in the dark corridors in white socks and saddle oxfords, and there were round, sweet syllables on their tongues. Time receded into Genesis on an autumn day in 1946.

West of Jemez Pueblo there is a great red mesa, and in the folds of the earth at its base there is a canyon, the dark red walls of which are sheer and shadow-stained; they rise vertically to a remarkable height. You do not suspect that the canyon is there, but you turn a corner and the walls contain you; you look into a corridor of geologic time. When I went into that place I left my horse outside, for there was a strange light and quiet upon the walls, and the shadows closed upon me. I looked up, straight up, to the serpentine strip of the sky. It was clear and deep, like a river running across the top of the world. The sand in which I stood was deep, and I could feel the cold of it through the soles of my shoes. And when I walked out, the light and heat of the day struck me so hard that I nearly fell. On the side of a hill in the plain of the Hissar I saw my horse grazing among sheep. The land inclined into the distance, to the Pamirs, to the Fedchenko Glacier. The river which I had seen near the sun had run out into the endless ether above the Karakoram range and the Plateau of Tibet.

Señora Tosa. She is perhaps the first
person I saw at Jemez.

FOUR

1

I WAS TOLD ON THE telephone that the Jemez Day School had burned down in the night. The fire had burned through the night; there was nothing to be done about it.

The day school had been my home; it was the last, best home of my childhood, and I went right away to see what was left of it. There was nothing but a shell, a ghost. It seemed already an ancient ruin in the pale January morning. What a strange and solemn experience it was for me, one that I can neither express nor understand. I had the sense that I was looking for myself there among the ashes.

My parents lived and taught at the Jemez Day School for more than a quarter of a century. It was my home from the time I was twelve until I ventured out to seek my fortune in the world. My most vivid and deeply cherished boyhood memories are centered upon that place. I used to wonder what would become of the day school in time, whether or not it would survive as I knew it, bearing always something of my presence, my having been there. It never occurred to me that it might be destroyed by fire.

Now the interior was gutted; there was only so much charred rubble. I was stunned to see it so, as if a dream too large to bear had fallen down on me. Other people were there, too, looking on in silence: a government inspector, a teacher, a man of the village who had brought his small son along, perhaps to reckon on the ravages of fire, to learn a lesson where so many lessons had been learned. I wanted to tell them what it meant to me, this place and this scene: that the fire had somehow involved me personally, that it had brought an end to some of the immediate properties of my remembered youth and the homely stage upon which I had played out my adolescence. I wanted to say that this was a pyre of matters and moments that were peculiarly mine. But of course I did not say these things at last. At last there was nothing to say.

The two classrooms and the teachers' quarters were housed together in the one building. Just there, in that room full of black debris, I had seen my mother on innumerable occasions, seated at her desk, the rows of Jemez children aligned before her. (Now and then, when I came to pay a visit, I spoke to the children in their own Tanoan dialect, and they were delighted and drew me at once into the language beyond my depth.) Again, there I stood, in that very doorway, and admitted for a dime those who came on Friday nights to see the movies which my father projected on the wall of the adjoining room. They were quite wonderful movies: *Stagecoach, My Darling Clementine*, a whole festival of Laurel and Hardy. My first published poem was written just there, at one of the second graders' desks, one night when I had come home from college for the weekend. And there was our living room. The old brick fireplace withstood the heat of countless fires, including this one, though the mantel is burned away. (How many times have I reached upon that mantel for something, a pencil or a key? There, in my day, stood a hundred-year-old Seth Thomas clock which chimed the hours of my growing up.) I suppose that I must have carried a thousand armloads of wood to that fireplace—and as many scuttles full of coal. I spent many an evening gazing into the blue and yellow flames that flowered there. What an irony, now, to think so longingly of fires on winter's nights just there, just there.

And there the kitchen where I sat at the table and did my homework or ironed out the wrinkles of my life over cocoa and cake. There, at that window one night, I saw a group of old men on the moonlit road, running in ceremonial garb after witches. It is a vision that I shall carry in my mind as long as I live.

The Jemez Day School was built in 1929. It stood for less than fifty years, not a long life for a building. In the last few years—since my time there—the character of the school changed remarkably. Other buildings grew up around it. The old storerooms, the coalbin, and the garage in which stood the Kohler engine that generated our light and heat, were converted into gleaming modern compartments— a cafeteria, a clinic, bathrooms. The old porch, where my parents and I sat talking or listening to the sounds of the village on summer evenings, became an administrative office, and a kindergarten now stands on the sandy reach where I pastured my horses. No, not a long time. But in that span and in that place were invested many days of my life, and many of the very best, I believe.

My parents hankered after the old, sacred world from which we had come to Hobbs, as I did, too, without clearly knowing it. If you

119

have ever been to the hogans in Canyon de Chelly, or to a squaw dance near Lukachukai—if you have ever heard the riding songs in the dusk, or the music of the *yei bichai*—you will never come away entirely, but a part of you will remain there always; you will have found an old home of the spirit.

It happened that a teaching job opened up at the Cañoncito Day School on the Navajo reservation between Albuquerque and Gallup, and my mother decided to take it. Sooner or later there would be two positions somewhere, my mother was assured, and my father and I would join her. And so it came about, sooner than could have been expected. In a matter of days my parents were offered the two-teacher day school at Jemez Pueblo, some fifty miles north and west of Albuquerque, due west of Santa Fe, in the canyon country beneath the Jemez Mountains. None of us had ever been there before. My mother went there directly from Cañoncito, and my father and I collected our things and set out from Hobbs with a man whom my father had hired to move us in his truck. That was in September, 1946. We arrived late at night, having got lost and gone nearly to Cuba, New Mexico, on the Farmington road. I can still see that dirt and gravel road in the light of the headlamps, white, with the black night on either side, the blue, black-dotted dunes in the moonlight beyond, and the bright stars. Rabbits and coyotes crossed the road. There was no pavement then on our way beyond Bernalillo, and for the last thirty miles or so the little truck bounced and rattled into the wild country. I could remember having, years before, when I was small, driven with my father across Snake Flats, on the Navajo. In heavy rain or snow the road was impassable, and we had had to wait until late at night, when it was frozen hard, in order to drive upon it.

The next morning I woke up, and there was a great excitement in me, as if something strange and wonderful had happened in the night: I had somehow got myself deep into the world, deeper than ever before. Perhaps I really expected nothing, and so I could not have been disappointed, but I do not believe that. Anyway, no expectation could possibly have been equal to the brilliance and exhilaration of that autumn New Mexican morning. Outside I caught my breath on the cold, delicious air of the Jemez Valley, lying out at six thousand feet. Around me were all the colors of the earth that I have ever seen. As I think back to that morning, there comes to my mind a sentence in Isak Dinesen: "In the highlands you woke up in the morning and thought: Here I am, where I ought to be."

The valley slopes down from north to south, and the pueblo lies down in the depth of it, on the east bank of the shallow Jemez River. Some four miles to the north is the little settlement of Cañon, nestled in sheer formations of red rock, and beyond is the long, deep San Diego Canyon, rising sharply up to the dark-timbered walls of the Jemez Range, to the Valle Grande, which is the largest caldera in the world, and to the summit above eleven thousand feet, from which you can look across the distance eastward to the Sangre de Cristos. Five miles to the south is the village of San Ysidro, where the valley loses its definition and the earth fans out in wide reaches of white, semi-arid plains. The junction at San Ysidro is as close as you can come to Jemez Pueblo in a Trailways bus; State Road 44 runs south and east to Bernalillo, north and west to Cuba, Bloomfield, and Farmington, near my old home of Shiprock. The east side of the valley is a long blue mesa, which from the pueblo seems far away, and in my years there I never covered the whole distance between, though I rode around for a thousand miles, it may be, on horseback. The conformation of that mesa is the rule of a solar calendar; for as long as anyone knows the Jemez people have lived their lives according to the ranging of the sun as it appears every day on that long, level skyline. Closer on the west, across the river, the valley is sharp-edged, given up abruptly to a high, broken wall—to walls beyond walls—of many colors. There is the red mesa upon which are still to be found

121

the ancient ruins of Zia, there the white sandstone cliffs in which is carved the old sacred cave of the Jemez Snake Clan, and there are pink and purple hills, ascending to the lone blue mountain in the northwest, where there are bears and mountain lions as well as deer and where once, in living memory, there were wolves.

The character of the landscape changed from hour to hour in the day, and from day to day, season to season. Nothing there of the earth could be taken for granted; you felt that Creation was going on in your sight. You see things in the high air that you do not see farther down in the lowlands. In the plains you can see farther than you have ever seen, and that is to gain a great freedom. But in the high country all objects bear upon you, and you touch hard upon the earth. The air of the mountains is itself an element in which vision is made acute; eagles bear me out. From my home of Jemez I could see the huge, billowing clouds above the Valle Grande, how, even motionless, they drew close upon me and merged with my life.

At that time the pueblo numbered about a thousand inhabitants. It was then a very close, integrated community, concentrated upon the plaza, with narrow streets and a number of buildings, in each of which several families lived. The population thinned out in proportion as you moved away from the plaza, though there were many *ranchitos*, especially on the north and west, where the fields were numerous. A few families kept houses across the river in order to be near the farthest fields, and in the summer they journeyed there in wagons and set themselves up, but when the harvest was in they returned to the village. It is a principle of their lives that the pueblo people move ever towards the center. Their sacred ceremonies are performed in the plaza, and in the kiva there. On the surrounding edge of the pueblo were numerous corrals, orchards, and little gardens of corn, chili, melons, and squash. In the autumn, and most of all in the late afternoons, the sun set a wonderful glow upon the adobe walls, in the colors of copper and gold, and brilliant red strings of chilies hung from the vigas. There was no electricity at Jemez in 1946, and no water in the village, other than that which was pumped from the ground by means of windmills, three or four in all. The men diverted water from the river for their fields; all about the farmlands was an intricate network of irrigation ditches. And of course much depended upon the rains, and the snowfalls in the mountains. Water is a holy thing in the pueblos; you come to understand there how the heart yearns for it. You learn to watch the level of the river, and when the rain comes, you hold your face and your hands up to it. There were perhaps three pickup trucks in the pueblo then, and no automobiles that I can remember. Everyone went abroad in wagons and on horseback, or else they walked; and frequently the boys and men, even the very young and the very old, ran about on their feet. The pueblo men have always been very good long-distance runners.

By car, unless you happened to come on the old road from San Ysidro, which was by and large a horse-and-wagon path, you entered the pueblo on the east side, on a street (that word is not entirely appropriate—"street," as Americans in cities and suburbs think of that word, does not truly indicate any of the ancient ways of that place, but it will have to do) which curved around the front of the Pueblo Church. The church was a large adobe building with three old Spanish bells in the façade and a burial ground in the yard. The Roman Catholic churches of the pueblos are so old, many of them, that they seem scarcely to impose an alien aspect upon the native culture; rather, they seem themselves almost to have been appropriated by that culture and to express it in its own terms. The church at Jemez has not the rich, rude beauty of the ruin at Acoma, or of even the church at Zia, say; nonetheless there is considerable strength and dignity in it. The extant parish records go back to 1720.

There you came to a fork. If you continued on around the church

123

you were on the way to the San Diego Mission, which lay out on the west side of the village; there was the mission school, which went through the first eight grades, the residence house of the nuns who taught there, the rectory with its adjoining chapel, where lived the Franciscan parish priest and his assistants, and the United States Post Office. If you bore to the left you were on the way to the Jemez Day School, on the southwestern corner of the pueblo, and on the old wagon road to San Ysidro.

The day school was a large stucco building in the pueblo style, not unlike the Pueblo Church in certain respects, especially that part of it which was officially the "school"; it had vigas, a dozen large windows along the south wall, admitting light into the classrooms, and a belfry in front. The two classrooms, situated end to end, were of about the same size; each could accommodate about thirty pupils comfortably. The highest enrollment during my parents' tenure there was sixty-eight. The front classroom was my mother's; she taught the beginners (who comprised a kind of kindergarten class, and most of whom could not speak English when they came), the first, the second, and the third graders. In the other classroom my father, who was the principal, taught the fourth, fifth, and sixth graders. My parents were assisted by a "housekeeper," a Jemez woman whose job it was to clean the classrooms, supervise the playground, and prepare the noon meal for the children. Frequently she assisted as an interpreter as well. On the opposite side of the building were the teachers' quarters, roughly equivalent in size to one of the classrooms. There were a living room, a kitchen, two bedrooms, and a bath. There was also a screened porch in front, where it was comfortable to sit in the good weather, and another, much smaller, in back; the latter we used largely for storage; there was our woodbox, convenient to the living room, in which there was a fireplace, and to the kitchen, in which, when we moved there, there was an old wood-burning range. In the living room there was a door which opened upon my mother's classroom, and beside this door a wall telephone with two bells and a crank. We shared a party line with the San Diego Mission and the Jemez Trading Post; there were no other telephones in the pueblo; we answered to two long rings and one short.

There were two other buildings on the school grounds. In one of these was the garage, a storeroom, the coalbin, and a makeshift clinic to which Government Service doctors and nurses came periodically to treat the ailing people of the village; in the other there lived at various times chickens, ducks, and turkeys—and for some months the meanest rooster I have ever known; perhaps his name was Oliver Blount, or Thaddeus Waring. Once, after he had attacked me viciously, I knocked him unconscious with a stone. It was a lucky throw, through the fence, and the cowardice of it lay heavy on me for days afterwards. Oh, you are a mean one, Blount, but you are not so mean as I.

A white fence encircled the school. We had in back a windmill and a water tank, and beyond the white fence there was a large field where later my father and I built a corral and shelter for Pecos, my strawberry roan quarter horse, my darling, my delight. The grounds were bare at first, except for five elms which shaded the teacherage, but later my mother planted tamaracks and Russian olives along the fence; they flourished. Along the north side of the day school ran the road to the river, which was about a half mile west, and upon that road we saw much of the commerce of the village from our kitchen windows. And just across that road lived our closest neighbors, the Tosa family.

I resumed my seventh-grade studies at the mission school. I loved to walk there in the morning, for on the way there were interesting and beautiful things to see. The old man Francisco Tosa kept a flock of sheep, and as I passed by his corrals I often saw him there, tending

My mother in her classroom at Jemez.
She loved it there; she loved every
moment of that long time.

them. He always greeted me heartily in Spanish, and there was much good humor in him. There are certain people whom you are simply glad to see at any moment, anywhere, for they hold themselves to their lives very peacefully and know who they are, and Francisco Tosa was one of these. He wore a red kerchief around his head, his long white hair tied with a finely woven band in a queue, and over this a big straw hat. He cut a very handsome figure, I thought, and he was a medicine man. It is the part of a medicine man to be inscrutable, if not austere—or so it has always seemed to me—but Francisco did not live up to such an image; he was jovial and serene, and he personified some old, preeminent ethic of pueblo life. I crossed over a little stream bed, where sometimes there was water, sometimes not; when it was there, animals came to drink, and the women washed corn in their yucca baskets. I passed through a lovely orchard near a house in which I liked to imagine there lived a witch; it strikes me that I never saw anyone there, and yet it was a fine old house and well kept; everything about it was in place. And I bent down through strands of barbed wire and was then in the yard of the mission school.

I was in that position of great advantage again, that of being alone among my classmates at home in the English language. From another and more valid point of view, it was a position of disadvantage. I had no real benefit of instruction at the mission school, and consequently I remember very little of what happened during those hours when I sat at my desk, listening to the nuns. One day Sister Mary Teresa put us the question "Which country is larger, the United States or the Soviet Union?" Child's play. Called upon, I replied confidently that the Soviet Union was certainly the larger country. "No," said Sister Mary Teresa, "the United States is quite a lot bigger than the Soviet Union." And to prove her point she held up two maps, one of each country, which bore no relation to each other in terms of scale; but the two countries were there irrefutably juxtaposed in our sight, and sure enough, the United States appeared to be larger by a third than the Soviet Union. The force of this logic made a great impression on me, and I have not forgotten it. There was a little parable on the nature of faith, I believe; it was as if I had been witness to a miracle.

And yet it was for me a time of great learning. As I think of it, it was the most common and essential kind of learning, purely natural and irresistible. Life itself is the object of such learning; it is not so much the achievement of study; rather it is simply the construction of an idea, an idea of having existence, place in the scheme of things. I learned of my life at Jemez in the way that I had learned to talk at the age of two, in the ordinary course of things, according to the nature of my mind. But it is *my* mind and *my* experience that concern me here, and that is a unique equation. Who was there among the moments in that legendary world? It was I.

And what moments there were.

In November the air turned very cold, and there were flurries of snow in the sky. The colors of the valley became soft and suffused, as if a mist or a thin smoke lay still upon the landscape. The motion of life quickened remarkably: wagons rattled by on the roads, the horses hurrying and blowing steam; fires blazed everywhere in the village; and at the gray end of the day the voice of the village governor rang out over the housetops in a rolling, deep-throated chant; and then the clear winter night came up and the singing began; it seemed that the thousand stars guttered to the drums.

The activity in the pueblo reached a peak on the day before the Feast of San Diego, November twelfth. It was on that day, an especially brilliant day in which the winter held off and the sun shone like a flare, that Jemez became one of the fabulous cities of the world. In the preceding days the women had plastered the houses, many of them, and they were clean and beautiful like bone in the high light;

the strings of chilies at the vigas had darkened a little and taken on a deeper, softer sheen; ears of colored corn were strung at the doors, and fresh cedar boughs were laid about, setting a whole, wild fragrance on the air. The women were baking bread in the outdoor ovens. Here and there men and women were at the woodpiles, chopping, taking up loads of firewood for their kitchens, for the coming feast. Even the children were at work: the little boys looked after the stock, and the little girls carried babies about. There were gleaming antlers on the rooftops, and smoke arose from all the chimneys.

About midday the Navajos began to arrive. And they seemed *all* to come, as a whole people, as if it was their racial destiny to find at last the center of the world, the place of origin, older than *tsegi*, among the rocks. From the yard of the day school I looked southward, along the road to San Ysidro, and there was a train of covered wagons, extending as far as I could see. All afternoon the caravan passed by, shimmering in the winter light, its numberless facets gleaming, the hundreds of wagon wheels turning in the dust, in slow and endless motion. Never have the Navajos seemed a more beautiful people to me, for they bore about them the cherished memories of my childhood. This old man, had he not once told us the way to Klagetoh? That beautiful woman, had she not been a schoolgirl at Chinle? They were resplendent. The old people and the children peered out from beneath the canopies, dark-skinned and black-eyed, nearly tentative in the shadows, beautiful in the way that certain photographic negatives are beautiful, dimly traced with light. The outriders were men and women and youths on handsome horses in glossy leather trappings and rich saddle blankets, the men in big hats and fine boots and bright silk and satin shirts, the women in velveteen blouses, long, pleated skirts, and red moccasins. They all wore silver and turquoise and coral—concha belts, necklaces, bracelets, and rings which flashed and glinted and gleamed in the sun. And their voices,

129

as I hear them even now—the singing and the laughter—carried along the train like a long, rising and falling woodwind music; it is a sound that I have heard among bristlecones, or upon the walls of the old ruin of Giusewa. A dog or two followed after each of the wagons, keeping closely in place. The Navajo dogs are solitary creatures. I believe that they assume very early the reserve and nobility of the people with whom they live and they consist in that assumption. They are shepherds, and they know their sheep in the way that an eagle knows its nest; and when they have not their sheep they concentrate themselves in the shadows of the wagons.

Some of the men of Jemez rode out to meet the Navajos. John Cajero was one of them. He was then a man in his prime, a Tanoan man, agile and strong in his mind and body, and he was a first-rate horseman. He was mounted on a good-looking gray quarter horse, which he handled closely and well, and he cut a fine figure upon it in his blue shirt and red headband, his manner easy and confident. He singled out old friends among the Navajos, and soon there was a cluster of riders holding up on the side of the road, convened in a high mood of fellowship and good humor—and a certain rivalry. Then John Cajero was holding the coils of a rope in his hands, shaking out a loop. Suddenly he leaned forward and his horse bolted into the road between two of the wagons, nearly trampling over a dog; the dog lunged away with a yelp and ran at full speed, but the horse was right upon it, bunched in motion, and the rope flashed down and caught the dog up around its hips and set it rolling and twisting in the sand, jerking it up then into the air and slamming it down hard, as the horse squatted, jamming its hooves in the earth, its whole weight cracking against the bit. And John Cajero played out a little of the rope from his saddle, and the dog slithered out of the noose and ran ahead, its tail between its legs, and went crouching and wary under its wagon. John Cajero laughed, and the others, too, though their laughter was brittle, I thought, and the Navajos watched evenly the

130

performance, the enactment of a hard joke, and considered precisely what it was worth. There was a kind of trade in this, a bartering of nerve and arrogance and skill, of elemental pride. Then, getting down from his horse, John Cajero drew a dollar bill from his pocket, folded it once lengthwise, and stuck it down in the sand. He gestured to the others; it was a beckoning, an invitation, but I did not understand at first what he meant them to do. He swung himself up into the saddle and gestured again, pointing down to the money on the ground. No one moved; only they were watchful, and he urged his horse away, prancing, a little distance. Then he turned the horse around and set it running—or loping, rather, not fast, but easily, evenly—and reached down from the saddle for the dollar bill. It seemed that his fingers brushed it, but he could not take hold of it, for the stride of the horse was broken slightly at the crucial moment. It was the barest miss—and a beautiful, thrilling thing to see—and he was upright in the saddle again, his motion and the motion of the horse all of a piece. I was watching him so intently that I did not at first see the girl. She came from nowhere, a lithe, lovely Navajo girl on a black horse. She was coming up fast in John Cajero's dust, faster than he had come, and her horse was holding steady in a long, loping stride, level and low. When I saw her she was already hanging down nearly the whole length of her arm from the saddle horn, her knee cocked and her long back curved like a bow, her shoulders close against the deep chest of the horse; she swung her left arm down like a scythe, and up, holding the dollar bill with the tips of her fingers until it was high over her head, and she was standing straight in the stirrups, and her horse did not break stride. And in that way she rode on, past John Cajero, along the wagon train and into the village, having stolen the show and the money, too, going in beauty, trailing laughter. Later I looked for her among the camps, but I did not find her. I imagined that her name was Desbah Yazzie and that she looked out for me from the shadows.

Later in the dusky streets I walked among the Navajo camps, past the doorways of the town, from which came the good smells of cooking, the festive sounds of music, laughter, and talk. The campfires rippled in the crisp wind that arose with evening and set a soft yellow glow on the ground, low on the adobe walls. Mutton sizzled and smoked above the fires; fat dripped into the flames; there were great black pots of strong coffee and buckets full of fried bread; dogs crouched on the rim of the light, the many circles of light; and old men sat hunched in their blankets on the ground, in the cold shadows, smoking, giving almost nothing—only a vague notion—of themselves away. Long into the night the fires cast a glare over the town, and I could hear the singing, until it seemed that one by one the voices fell away, and one remained, and then there was none. On the very edge of sleep I heard coyotes in the hills.

The next day, November twelfth, began with mass at the Pueblo Church. It seemed that the whole town, and all of the visitors, were there, packed into the pews, in the aisle, spilling out of the doors, standing in the *campo santo*. The bright sunlight streamed into the windows, and everyone was dressed in bright colors. The candles on the altar were bright and shone on the bright gilt of the old *santos* and *retablos*. And outside the windows and walls of the church and the village were bright, and the air of the valley was bright as glass, and it was a deep, bright day in the bright November of New Mexico. And after mass the governor spoke in the door of the church, and all of the people formed a procession and moved in a bright throng through the streets to the plaza, to the dancing of the Pecos horse, to the high, constant rattle of a drum.

The street on the north side of the plaza had become a trade fair. There were beautiful things to see: Navajo blankets and silverwork and turquoise, Zia and Santa Ana pottery, Jicarilla baskets; and especially brisk was the trade in perishables; the Jemez people traded their sweet, heavy loaves of *sotobalough* for mutton from Torreon, for apples and melons from Cañon, San Ysidro, and Vallecitos.

As my parents and I wandered along this old north street, observing all that was going on, we were invited to feast in the home of Joe R. Toya, who was to become our close friend and whose children and grandchildren were to graduate from the day school during my parents' tenure there. It is the custom at Jemez that, on the feast days, all of the houses are open to guests; anyone might enter and be welcome—and eat his fill—whether he has been formally invited or not; nonetheless it is a considerable honor to be invited especially, and so it was with us; we were treated royally. The house was immaculate, the earthen floors swept clean as a bone, with everything in its place. A little, long-fingered fire burned evenly in the corner fireplace of the front room. Almost at once we were ushered into the kitchen, where there was a large table laden with food, around which there sat four or five guests, all from out of town, according to their dress, all congenial to us, and shy. Places were made straight away for us, and we were bidden to eat. The food, which was kept hot and unendingly replenished before us, was quite wonderful to see, to smell, and to taste. There were three principal dishes, traditional in the pueblos, stews of rich and distinctive flavor. The first of these was a mild corn stew, that which is called *posole*, made with dried corn (something like hominy), pork bones, and a small amount of chili; the soup of this stew is thin and delicious, and it is among the dishes that I like best in the world. There is no Christmas but that I crave this spicy, smoking Indian *posole*. The second was a thicker soup of chili and beef, brick red in color and decidedly hotter to the taste. And the third was made also of chili and beef and was essentially a deep red chili paste, *con carne*, that burned the mouth and caused perspiration to rise from all the pores of the brow. When I first ate of this dish my whole being cried out for water—I should have given anything for even a spoonful of cold water—but there was none; rather there was

133

only coffee, and it was so hot that it scalded my tongue. Thus did I learn once and for all to eat at the Jemez feasts in the Jemez style, to take bread and dip it into the fiery food and to taste of it delicately, with deliberation and particular respect. I believe that the good, substantial *sotobalough* exists to this very purpose; the moist, sweet, hard-crusted, soft-centered and porous bread is a sop than which there is none better. In addition there was on the table a great variety of canned fruits, breads and *biscochitos,* pies and cakes. Mrs. Toya baked excellent apple pies. We were admonished again and again to "eat good," and that we did. But later, when we went outside again, we were invited to feast in another home, then another, and another, and it seemed that in the interest of diplomacy we could not refuse. In the years at Jemez we were required to negotiate many times an apparent hunger, to exercise fine discretions and deceits. And in this much there was salvation, at least propriety and reprieve. In one of the homes there was a wedding that day. Mary Fragua, the daughter of our housekeeper, Avelina, and a singularly beautiful girl, was married to a young, good-looking man of the pueblo. An old Spanish man of Cañon appeared there in a rumpled black suit and made a sweet, squeaking music on his little violin. Mary wore the traditional manta and white leggings, and she was tall and slender for a pueblo girl, and her deep eyes were dark and dancing and her face was round and radiant, and there grew up in me an admiration for her that was strung between love and lust, and I was full of benevolence and misery.

Through the afternoon the dance went on in the universe. The plaza was thronged with people of every description; they clung there to the adobe walls, looking on; they stood on the housetops, high against the winter sky; and they gave themselves up to the motion and the music of the holy world which was centered there. The dancers came forth in long files of concentrated men and women, first one and then the other of the great Jemez clans, the Turquoise and

134

the Squash, their bodies blue and yellow, taut and tethered to the drums, their feet shaking the hard earth. In them was unspeakable calm and intensity, and these were, I thought and think, unaccountable and unaccountably the same thing. They described every impulse, the whole rhythm of the turning of the earth, the returning of time upon it forever.

Dusk was falling at five o'clock, when the dancing came to an end, and on the way home alone I bought a Navajo dog. I bargained for a while with the thin, wary man whose dog it was, and we settled on a price of five dollars. It was a yellow, honest-to-goodness, great-hearted dog, and the man gave me a bit of rope with which to pull it home. The dog was not large, but neither was it small. It was one of those unremarkable creatures that one sees in every corner of the world. If there were only thirty-nine dogs in Creation, this one would be the fourth, or the thirteenth, or the twenty-first, the archetype, the common denominator of all its kind. It was full of resistance, and yet it was ready to return in full measure my deep, abiding love. I could see that. It needed only, I reasoned, to make a small adjustment in its style of life, to shift the focus of its vitality from one frame of reference to another, in order to be perfectly at home with me. Even as it was nearly strangled on the way, it wagged its bushy tail happily all the while. That night I tied the dog up in the garage, where there was a warm, clean pallet, wholesome food, and fresh water, and I bolted the door. And the next morning the dog was gone, as in my heart of hearts I knew it would be, I believe. I had read such a future in its eyes. It had gnawed the rope in two and squeezed through a vent in the door, an opening much too small for it, as I had thought. But, sure enough, where there is a will there is a way, and the Navajo dog was possessed of one indomitable will. I was crushed at the time, but strangely reconciled, too, as if I had perceived some truth beyond billboards. The dog had done what it had to do, had behaved exactly as it must, had been true to itself and to the sun and moon. It knew its place in the order of things, and its place was away out there in the tracks of a wagon, going home. In the mind's eye I could see it at that very moment, miles away, plodding in the familiar shadows, its tail drooping a little after the harrowing night, but wagging, in its dog's mind contemplating the wonderful ways of mankind.

And on that same harrowing night I saw witches. Some children came to tell us that the witches were about. "Come, we will show you," they said, and they led us outside and pointed with their chins into the night. There, at ground level and far away, were lights, three or four, moving here and there, back and forth. The children watched very solemnly, without alarm, and I understood at once that they were not playing tricks; neither did they care one way or another what I thought of what I saw; only they imagined that I might find it interesting to see witches. You are deceived, I thought; there are men with flashlights, running around in the distance, that is all. But then one of the lights flew suddenly into the air and, like a shooting star, moved across the whole dome of the sky. After midnight Mary Fragua, or whatever her name had become that day, came banging on the door and screaming, "My husband is going to kill me! My husband is going to kill me!" My father let her in and calmed her down, and she went presently to sleep on the divan in our living room. All night long I made trips to the bathroom, that I might switch on the light and see in the flood of it her reclining, foreshortened form, barefooted, beautiful and forsaken, rising and falling, rising and falling.

And the next year there were fewer covered wagons, fewer men and women on horseback. And the next there was relatively little to see on the old wagon road, but the people came in on the high road in cars and trucks. And I think often and with great longing of that first Feast of San Diego in my life at Jemez, that pageant that happened upon me like a dream: say that it was good to see, that it will not be seen again.

The Christmas dances were held indoors, and I went and sat among the many people, and the drum resounded in the room like thunder, and the dancers swayed above me, their shadows thrown up on the white walls, lurching and trembling, and the voices of the singers careened on my soul. On Christmas Eve children came to build a bonfire in front of the day school, and there were bonfires everywhere in the village. After the midnight mass at the Pueblo Church a procession bore the statue of the Christ child to the home of the *patrones*. And there we feasted. Later, in a recollection of my Christmases at Jemez, I wrote a story in which I could see almost everything of that special time, that special place.

Dypaloh. The village lies in all seasons like a scattering of smooth stones in a wide fold of the sandy earth. The land rises away to the north, where again it falls in a great round bowl full of marshes and of grass. On three sides of the great meadow there are blue mountains and deep woods, where wild animals abound. It is said of this wilderness that it is as old as the moon and has no end in time.

Once there was a poor mute boy whose name was Tolo. In three seasons of the year he lived with his mother and father in the village, but in the summers he went to the house of his grandfather in the great meadow at the foot of the mountains. Tolo loved above all to be with his grandfather, for the old man was good to him and told him wonderful stories. But when Tolo was still a child his grandfather died, and the boy no longer went to the meadow. Still, he remembered what sort of place it was, and he lived there in his dreams.

He remembered that his grandfather had known the creatures of the mountains. The summer before he died, the old man had taken

137

Tolo to the high rim of the great meadow. They sat at the foot of the mountains, near dark woods of cedar and pine, where they could see out across the long, rolling plain.

As the light darkened in the late afternoon they saw an eagle in the distance. It soared in high, wide arcs above the land, and the setting sun struck a dark fire upon its wings. At dusk a great bull elk came slowly down from the woods to drink from a spring in the marsh, and it stood like a huge black rock among the reeds in the low mist of the water until the night grew up around it. Then moonlight filled the meadow, and they heard the long wail of a wolf upon the slopes.

Time and again Tolo wanted to tell his parents of what he had seen and heard, but because he had no voice he lived alone with his memories, dreaming. At such times his grandfather came into his thoughts, and then loneliness fell upon him, and he wept.

But now it was Christmas Eve, and there was a great excitement in Tolo's house, for this year his parents were to be the patrons of the Christ child. Even now his mother was preparing a feast for the people of the village, for after the first mass on Christmas morning they would come in procession to pay their respects and to kneel in adoration before the statue of the Holy Infant. And now, too, his father was building a shrine in a corner of the room where Tolo slept, and Tolo gathered evergreen boughs and made ornaments with which to decorate it.

All day Tolo waited, dreaming of the Christ child. He had worked hard, and he was very tired. At last everything was ready, and it was time to go to the church, for the midnight mass was about to begin.

The church stood at the very center of the village. Its high, thick walls were smooth and earth-colored, and there were three ancient bells above the door. Inside, the altar shone with the light of many candles. All about there were lovely things to see, paintings and prayer plumes, ribbons and wreaths. At one side of the altar stood a small, perfect tree, its ornaments shimmering in the soft light, and at the other a crêche, in which the statue of the Christ child lay in a bed of straw.

Down the long aisle came the good people of the village, old men in beautiful blankets, women in their fringed shawls, children in their new Christmas finery. In one corner, near the door, a fire roared in an old iron stove. The metal glowed red, like an ember, and a cheerful warmth radiated to all the walls. The music of the bells was everywhere. How good it was to come into this holy place from the raw winter night!

Tolo and his parents sat near the front at a place of honor, where they could see directly into the crêche. The little statue of the Christ child was very beautiful, and for a time Tolo could look at nothing else. But after a while he began to grow sleepy and to wander in his thoughts. He remembered his grandfather and became very lonely. His loneliness grew so large that he wanted to cry, but at the same time he was glad to dream. It was as if the old man had returned to him. Indeed, his grandfather's presence was there in the church, so real that Tolo wanted to turn around and look for him.

When the mass was ended, Tolo's mother went to the manger and took the Christ child in her arms; she sat with it cradled in her lap, and Tolo's father sat beside her. Then the people of the village came forward to kiss the statue. Tolo held back for a time, half asleep, and then he moved to the aisle. An old man in a blanket was kneeling before his mother. Tolo's eyes grew wide, for the old man appeared to be his grandfather. Yes, surely it was he! The boy hurried, trying to call out his grandfather's name, but he got caught up in the crowd of people, and then the old man was gone.

Outside, the people were forming the procession. Bonfires had been lighted, and they made a long, bright line through the streets to Tolo's house. The light flickered on the walls of the buildings, and shadows danced about. The night air was clean and cold, and there was a rich fragrance of cedar smoke. Tolo looked everywhere for his grandfather, but he could not find him.

The procession moved away, and Tolo joined at the end. Still he looked all about, running now and then to keep up, for the people were walking very quickly in the cold. Then, far ahead, he caught sight of his grandfather. The old man left the procession and turned into one of the dark streets. Tolo ran after him, trying again to call out, but when he reached the street the old man was already at the other end, moving like the shadow of a bird.

Tolo followed as best he could, but the shadow fled to the edge of the village and beyond. Then the light of the bonfires fell away, and Tolo was alone in the hills. He lost sight of the shadow, but he went on and on, calling out in his heart against the great silence of the night.

He ran, then walked, for a long time and became weary and numb with cold. The lights and sounds of the village were far behind, and the night took hold of him. Still he went on. At last he saw a faint glow in the distance, where the mountains rose up among the stars. As he approached he heard the sharp sound of wood crackling amid flames and smelled a thin, sweet smoke. Lo, there was a fire, like the bonfires of the village, on the rim of the great meadow.

The mountains were covered with snow, and the dark timber seemed to stand upon the slopes like a gathering of old men, huddled and quiet. Tolo knelt down on the bright, warm ground and held his hands open to the flames. "Thank you, grandfather," he said in his heart, but it seemed to him that his voice rang like a bell and made an echo among the trees. The fire filled him with gladness and peace, and he peered into it, dreaming.

After a while he heard something and looked up. The elk entered the circle of light and stood above Tolo, its eyes reflecting the whole of the night. Its antlers shone like shale, and its great body seemed as strong as the wilderness itself. The sight of the great beast filled his mind with wonder and delight, and Tolo dared not move, but he said, "Old Elk, please share with me the real gift of this fire." And again his voice seemed to resound like the wind.

In another moment a shadow moved upon them from the wood. The elk trembled, but only for a moment, and Tolo saw then that there was a long, crooked scar upon its flank, where the teeth of a wolf had long ago cut into the flesh. The wolf drew close and lay down in the light of the fire. The great creature seemed a very motion of the wilderness night, something made of the cold, invisible wind that moves forever among the trees. Tolo was amazed and said, "Old Wolf, please share with me the real gift of this fire."

There was then a sharp clatter of wings overhead, and only just then, for an instant, did the wolf stiffen and turn, and Tolo saw the ragged edge of the ear, where the talons of a great bird had long ago drawn blood. The eagle dropped down and settled in the firelight. It seemed a spirit of the wilderness sky, holding in its power the very force of the mountain storm. Tolo felt his heart beating hard within him, and he said, "Old Eagle, please share with me the real gift of this fire."

The hackles of the bird shone like gold in the moving light, and it shifted slightly on its feet, one of which was crooked, having long ago been broken in a trap. Each time he spoke, Tolo's voice rose like a song upon the deep silence of the night.

The boy, the bird, and the beasts made a circle of wonder and good will around the real gift of the fire, and beyond them were other, wider circles, made of the meadow, the mountains, and the starry sky, all the fires and processions, all the voices and silences of all the world. Tolo knew then that he had been led to the center of the Holy Season. He thought again of his grandfather, who he knew was near among the trees, and of his parents, and of the Christ child, who had come to live the twelve days of Christmas in his home. Never before had Tolo's heart been so full of joy.

The fire burned low, and when again he looked up the wild creatures had gone. He had shared with them the real gift of the fire, and they in turn had given of themselves to him and to each other. Across the great meadow he could see the coming dawn of Christmas

Day. He slept, and when once in the last shadow of the night he awoke, he lay at home in a warm pallet on the earthen floor below the shrine.

The only light in the room was that of a single votive candle; it guttered in the blue glass and cast a soft glow upon the head of the Christ child. Tolo turned and closed his eyes again, and he was no longer poor and mute. His spirit wheeled above the great meadow and the mountains, his loneliness was borne with the wild strength of a great elk, and he sang of his whole being with a voice that carried like the cry of a wolf. *Qtsedaba.*

The events of one's life take place, *take place.* How often have I used this expression, and how often have I stopped to think what it means? Events do indeed take place; they have meaning in relation to the things around them. And a part of my life happened to take place at Jemez. I existed in that landscape, and then my existence was indivisible with it. I placed my shadow there in the hills, my voice in the wind that ran there, in those old mornings and afternoons and evenings. It may be that the old people there watch for me in the streets; it may be so.

Late in February the people of Jemez turned out to clear the irrigation ditches. The sun appeared at a notch on the skyline; beyond that there was no sign of the spring; the snow was old and frozen fast on the north sides of the dunes, and in the air you could tell of more snow to come. And at dawn there was a foot race. The race was run over a long distance, towards the town, on the old San Ysidro road. I saw the runners pass in front of the day school in the cold gray morning, running evenly, their breath visible on the dark air, stripped to their waists. They ran without effort, or the ordinary effort had been translated into extraordinary terms; the running was ceremonial, emphatic, and was itself the measure of time. There were long successions in it, the runners again and again bearing down upon the

142

little cottonwood kick-stick, to place it on the broad, moccasined foot, to kick it high and away, wobbling in long arcs, running after it, not in a straight line along the road, but in zigzag lines across the road, back and forth; it is the way water rushes and dips, swirling along in the channels.

One day when the wind had got up and the weather had turned warm and the water was running fast I walked along the river, talking to myself and throwing stones against the bank opposite. After a time I was surprised to see many people coming from the village, in wagons, on horseback, and walking. I watched them come down to the crossing, a little way upstream from where I was standing, and I could not imagine what was going on. Then I saw my friend Eddie Loretto coming towards me on his horse. He pulled up and said to me, "Let's go; come with us." "Well, where?" I wanted to know. "Oh, we are going out to work. Come, help us." It was all right with me—I had nothing better to do, and I was very curious—and I climbed up on the horse behind Eddie and we followed after the others. We went out to the far fields below the west mesa, and there, in two large rectangles of freshly turned earth, we planted corn and melons, working all together, hard, like a great lot of ants. Soon the work was finished, and we sat down to eat in a cottonwood grove nearby. There was plenty of good food, and it was of a kind that I did not ordinarily see on the feast days. The main dish was a rabbit stew which was especially tasty. At first I sat down with Eddie and the members of his family, but in a little while Joe Baca, who held as I recall the office of war captain that year, came to me and invited me to sit with him and some other men who were seated in a circle at the center of the whole group. It was clear to me that I must accept this invitation, but I was reluctant and self-conscious, for it seemed to me that everyone was looking on in amusement. For a time I was ill at ease among those men whom I did not know. But they were very gracious to me and went out of their way to make me

143

comfortable. There is a great gift for hospitality in the Jemez people; welcome is intrinsic in them, and they judge others, I believe, by what is best in themselves. It happened after all that I was very pleased to talk and eat with these men, to laugh with them, to be alive in their company. And only later did I learn that I had been a highly honored, though unwitting, guest, that I had sat among the chief dignitaries of the town: the cacique, the governor, the lieutenant governor, and the war captain. Indeed, I had taken part in the ceremonial planting of the cacique's fields. The cacique, the chief of the tribe, presides over the matters of the pueblo, great and small, until he dies, and his position is one of singular honor and importance. Every year the people of Jemez plant and harvest his fields for him, and they give him a choice portion of the food which they obtain by means of hunting.

In June there was a "chicken pull." Some of the ablest riders of the village participated in this ancient sport, which is decidedly cruel, but also very exciting to see, inasmuch as it requires great skill. The riders convened on their horses at the west end of the plaza. Then someone, an official dressed ceremonially in white pants, a belted tunic, and moccasins, brought a rooster to the center of the plaza and buried it to its neck in sand; the miserable creature made a grotesque sight— the head of a bird, its yellow eyes blinking with fright, its neck craned, its comb flopping this way and that. Then one by one the riders rode running close upon it, each one leaning down to take hold of it and pull it from the ground. Most of the horses were poorly trained to the task, and some of the riders fell in the attempt, to the great delight of the lookers-on; but then one of them—perhaps it was John Cajero or Pasqual Fragua—took the rooster up and held it high in the air, its wings beating furiously. He turned then and walked his horse back to the west end, among the other riders, and one of these he began to beat heavily with the rooster about the head and shoulders. The man raised his arms to protect himself, but according

144

to the rules of the game he must stand his ground and try to catch the rooster up in the loop of his reins or under his arm. Inevitably he did so sooner or later, and the game became a tug of war; the adversaries then pulled the rooster apart (I hoped it was dead); its dismembered body was dropped on the ground and left to the dogs; and another poor creature was brought out, and the game was played again, and so on. In the late afternoon the affair was finished, and the women came out of the houses and threw water on the participants and spectators alike, I don't know why. In the years that I lived at Jemez the "chicken pull" was greatly diminished in its color and vitality; fewer and fewer participants turned out, and they seemed to be younger and less skillful each year, until it became at last a boys' game; but still it was a grisly business.

On the first of August, at dusk, the Pecos bull ran through the streets of Jemez, taunted by the children, chased by young boys who were dressed in outlandish costumes, most in a manner which parodied the curious white Americans who came frequently to see the rich sights of Jemez on feast days. This "bull" was a man who wore a mask, a wooden framework on his back covered with black cloth and resembling roughly a bull, the head of which was a crude thing made of horns, a sheepskin, and a red cloth tongue which wagged about. It ran around madly, lunging at the children; and they in turn were delighted with it, pretending great alarm. All this was played out amid much shouting and laughter. And then in the plaza appeared briefly another mask, the little horse of Pecos. This, too, was a man; he wore about his waist a covered framework in the shape of a horse, and he danced to the accompaniment of a drum, the drummer close by his side. But this mask is very different in character from that of the bull. It is indeed one of the most beautiful and dramatic figures in Jemez ceremony, a thing in which fine art and the elements of the sacred are brought together in a whole and profound expression. From the first time I saw the Pecos horse it has been fixed in my imagination, as if it had come to be there long before I knew it; such things are beheld, and in the same moment they are recognized, and they do not pass from the mind. The little head, with its delicate ears and black mane, was finely made. The frame of its body, draped round with a beautiful kilt, suggested perfectly its fine limbs, its temperament high-strung and imperative, its little round rump bunched and bouncing, its tail not flowing but shimmying. The man appeared to be mounted on the little horse, and he, too, was a beautiful and dramatic thing to see, a strange and almost ominous aspect of the mask, a black veil over his head, under a black hat. And all the while he danced to the high, hectic rattle of the drum, virtually in place, his motion translated into the pure illusion of the horse, the centaur quivering. And in the last light a holy man came out of one of the holy houses and sprinkled meal on the horse's head. Sometimes you look at a thing and see only that it is opaque, that it cannot be looked into. And this opacity is its essence, the very truth of the matter. So it was, for me, with the little Pecos horse mask. The man inside was merely motion, and he had no face, and his name was the name of the mask itself. Had I lifted the veil beneath the hat, there should have been no one and nothing to see.

The masks of the bull and the horse, along with an old statue of Our Lady of the Angels, are said to have been brought to Jemez by the survivors of Pecos, which place is now a ruin that lies some eighty miles to the south and east. The pueblo of Pecos was destroyed by a plague about 1840. The survivors, eighteen or twenty souls in all, came to Jemez and were taken in. From that time the blood of these two peoples has been mingled, and there are many Pecos elements now in Jemez tradition, including this observance, on August second, of the Feast of Our Lady of the Angels, who is called Porcingula.

The next day, after mass, the little statue Porcingula was borne in procession to the plaza and placed in a bower of evergreens there, and through the afternoon there was dancing and feasting, feasting in the homes of the Pecos descendants. I came to love this "Old Pecos Day," as it is called, above other feast days at Jemez. Perhaps it was because I, too, like those old immigrants, came there with my masks and was taken in.

And throughout the year there were ceremonies of many kinds, and some of these were secret dances, and on these holiest days guards were posted on the roads and no one was permitted to enter the village. My parents and I kept then to ourselves, to our reservation of the day school, and in this way, through the tender of our respect and our belief, we earned the trust of the Jemez people, and we were at home there.

Now as I look back on that long landscape of the Jemez Valley, it seems to me that I have seen much of the world. And I have been glad to see it, glad beyond the telling. But what I see now is this: If I should hear at evening the wagons on the river road and the voices of children playing in the cornfields, or if in the sunrise I should see the long shadows running out to the west and the cliffs flaring up in the light ascending, or if riding out on an afternoon cool with rain I should see in the middle distance the old man Francisco with his flock, standing deep in the colors and patterns of the plain, it would again be all that I could hold in my heart.

2

In North Street, near Turquoise Kiva, there was kept a golden eagle in a cage. Always, in passing, I spoke to it; and then, for a long moment, it held me fast in its regard, which was like doom. There was much shame between us, at the wire.

Lupe Lucero was a wizened child. He was very small and swarthy, with glittering black eyes and a shock of coarse black hair on his head. He was bandy-legged and much animated; something of the rooster Thaddeus Waring was in him, some wise and wary notion of the world. There was a slight deformity in the right side of his face, a thing which gave to him the grave look of a man who must deal with God before breakfast, the scowl of a theologian. And it suited him, I believe; it is the expression he would have chosen for himself, had there been a choice. It was in his nature, who could not himself have been taken by surprise, to take others by surprise, and all the time. He was of a mind to hold the world precisely at bay and in a delicate balance between delight and disdain. When he first came to the day school as a beginner he could speak only the Jemez language, but he was highly intelligent, and he learned very quickly. One day on the playground, when I was watching him (for he bore watching), the governor of the village came to the fence and asked Lupe in his native tongue where my father might be found. And after due consideration, Lupe replied, "I am sorry, my friend, but we speak only English here."

I did not and do not know his name. He was an old man who appeared at Jemez one winter. He was said to have come from one of the other pueblos, Zia, maybe, or San Felipe. He had a strong, heroic face, broad and dark and expressive—but expressive of what, exactly, I do not know. The talk of the village had it that he was *muy loco*, and perhaps it was so, but I was never convinced of it. His behavior was extraordinary, to be sure; he did things that other people in general did not think of doing. But I rather liked that in this old man and thought of it as his own business, after all. In any case I felt no compunction to account for him either to myself or to anyone else; he seemed to get on well enough in his particular way. He came to the day school on several occasions, walked right into our home without knocking, and stood for long moments before the fire, warming his

148

gnarled hands, saying nothing to anyone; or else he spoke out loudly, almost urgently, in a tongue that none of us knew or had ever heard before. And at such times he closed his eyes. I believe that he looked then inward upon his mind and saw there, and there only, such things as were real to him. One morning, when I stepped out into the raw January weather on my way to school, a truck sped by on the road in front of me, and in the bed of the truck were several young men laughing, jeering, and gesturing wildly. And in the dust in their wake rode the old man on a paint horse. He was standing in the stirrups and holding out both his arms in the attitude of Christ on the Cross, his face contorted in a scream and his long gray hair lying out flat on the wind, and the horse was running at full speed, bolting after the truck. It was a strange and breath-taking sight, something upon which to found a faith, it may be, a faith in the apparent, often beautiful, aberrations of this world.

The old man Francisco Tosa's daughter-in-law, Sefora, came every day to the day school for water, and her husband, Joe, brought wood from the mountains for our fires. Sefora was a beautiful woman, with fine pueblo features and a remarkably composed, gentle disposition. She was not jolly, as were many of the good women of Jemez; rather, she was very quiet and shy and sweet. The old ethnic reserve, which in others of her race, especially the men, made for a kind of formidable and exclusive nature, appeared in her as a soft and serene good will, a rich dignity and grace like beauty; indeed, beauty. She lived with her family directly across the river road, on the north side of the day school, and we could not have wished for a better neighbor. Very often she brought us the delicacies of her table, hot tortillas and beans, chili and tamales; and when she baked bread, she never failed to bring us one or two hot loaves. Joe, who was an excellent hunter, provided us with fresh venison, and sometimes bear meat. In the course of years my mother, especially, and Sefora Tosa became very close friends. When after all—after the good days and

149

bad, the weathers and harvests of twenty-six years, the coming and going of children at the day school—it was time for my parents to leave, it was hard for the two women to say goodbye. They must have seen much in each other's eyes. After I had been away for a long time and had become a man I returned to Jemez and called on Sefora Tosa. Her son Tony, whom I had known as a little boy at the day school, had only a few days before been killed in Vietnam. She wept softly to see me, and she thanked me for coming. I wanted to tell her how good it was to know her, to have known who and what she was to me through that past, pastoral time of my growing up in the neighborhood between us, the good realm in which we had come close together in our lives, but in that formal quiet of her grief I did not say it. And I want to say it now, that it may be said well, in love and remembrance.

Geese flew over the valley. Sometimes there were many geese, the long formations extending into the far reaches of the flat, curdled sky. One morning, on the river, thirty geese broke away from the water in a great commotion, scattering at first, then falling strangely into place, into silence. And then the silence was shattered as I saw in the corner of my eye the gun buck in my father's hands. And one of the trailing geese faltered and fell away from the angle and came wheeling down into the water. I picked it up and was deeply disturbed to see that it was alive. There was no resistance in it, neither fear, only a kind of calm and resignation I had never seen before, there in its eyes. Its body was heavy and slick with blood, and I carried it in my arms, close against me, and after a long time it died in my arms.

Quincy Tahoma was a Navajo artist, a watercolorist of very considerable talent. There is a Tahoma painting in my parents' home at Jemez Springs, a very fine one. It is the full figure of an old Navajo man at prayer. He stands on a rocky prominence in a wide, sunlit landscape, his legs apart, his head and arms uplifted. His buckskin horse stands below and behind him. His face and throat are drawn with age, but there is in his stature a remarkable vigor and strength. There is a quality of transcendence in the painting; that is its real subject, in fact; that lean old man is the stitch that holds the earth to the sky. Quincy himself had been disfigured by some disease of his youth; he had not the full use of his arms, and he held them always crooked slightly before him; they seemed disproportionately short, and I think that he could not extend them to their full length. He was otherwise a good-looking man of medium height with a certain sensitivity and intelligence in his face, and his smile was infectious; there was most often a deep delight in his eyes. He had been an orphan. Once he told my mother that when he was a baby he had been abandoned, left in the road to die. But an old man and woman found him and cared for him, and he grew up in their hogan at Blue Canyon. He liked to talk about his childhood; I believe that he thought it a strange and wonderful thing, like a miracle, that he was alive. There are certain people, those who have come close to death and know it, perhaps, in whom a sense of fate is predominant; they seem to walk always upon an edge and have a tentative hold upon their lives. So it was with Quincy Tahoma. His spirit was informed with this wonder, and he expressed his spirit in painting. He was one of those upon whom the character of Haske, in my mother's book *Owl in the Cedar Tree*, was modeled. Quincy came a number of times to Jemez in those days, in order to paint with my father. Each man greatly admired the other's work, and they learned much from each other. My father had already made his reputation as an artist, but just then he was beginning to be known as a successful teacher of art as well; the work which was produced by his students at the day school was being widely exhibited and acclaimed. I was always glad to see Quincy come into our home, for he brought a kind of cheerful excitement to it. Most often the two men set up a kind of makeshift studio in one of the rooms, and there they secluded themselves and worked for long hours; and from behind the door there came incessant laughter and buoyant talk. Now and then I was privileged to enter and observe. It excited me to see them at their work, to see how their fine, dark hands were set so patiently to the task, how delicately the brushes were drawn upon the picture plane, how colors and forms emerged in a moment. Once, looking on so at a painting which my father had begun, I thought: I see how it is that you proceed, that I am involved in this work, that you create a thing and it exists before my eyes, that in so doing you determine my point of view and confirm that I see and that I am, that therefore you create me, too. And then, towards the end of the day, Quincy Tahoma and my father went off into the mountains and took me with them, and there we cooked meat over an open fire until it was charred and crisp and delicious, and we saw the moon rise up in the black trees, and we laughed and laughed.

There was at Jemez a climate of the mind in which we, my parents and I, realized ourselves, understood who we were, not perfectly, it may be, but well enough. It was not our native world, but we appropriated it, as it were, to ourselves; we invested much of our lives in it, and in the end it was the remembered place of our hopes, our dreams, and our deep love.

My father looked after the endless paper work that came down from the many levels of the Bureau of Indian Affairs. In innumerable ways he worked with the people of the village and was their principal contact with the Government of the United States. When a boy or girl wanted to apply for admission to the Santa Fe Indian School or the Albuquerque Indian School, or when a man wanted to find work, or a woman to use the telephone to talk to her daughter in California, it was to my father that the petition was made. But first of all he was the man of the family. It was he who got up before daylight and went out to get wood and coal for the fires on winter mornings; it was he who dealt with the emergencies, great and small, of those years; and it was he who taught me such responsibilities as I learned then. One of these was to myself, and it was to dream. On winter evenings before the fire, or on summer nights on the porch, our home of Jemez was a place to dream, and my father dreamed much of his youth. He told me the stories of the coming-out people, of Mammedaty and of Guipagho, of Sayday, who wandered around and around. And very softly, as to himself, he sang the old Kiowa songs. And in all he went on with his real work, the making of paintings. He saw wonderful things, and he painted them well.

My mother has been the inspiration of many people. Certainly she has been mine, and certainly she was mine at Jemez, when inspiration was the nourishment I needed most. I was at that age in which a boy flounders. I had not much sense of where I must go or of what I must do and be in my life, and there were for me moments of great, growing urgency, in which I felt that I was imprisoned in the narrow quarters of my time and place. I wanted, needed to conceive of what my destiny might be, and my mother allowed me to believe that it might be worthwhile. We were so close, she and I, when I was growing up that even now I cannot express the feelings between us. I have great faith in words, but in this there are no words at last; there is only a kind of perfect silence—the stillness of a late autumn afternoon in the village and the valley—in which I listen for the sound of her voice. In a moment she will speak to me; she will speak my name.

One day my mother burned her hand. In a way it was my fault, for I had got in her way when she was carrying a hot pan to the table. It was a strange moment. She made a little cry, and I looked to see what was the matter. I stepped out of the way at once, but her hand was already burned. My mother said nothing about it—that was what seemed strange to me—but I had seen the pain in her face.

Many times she called me to the kitchen window to see something

153

of interest—horses running on the road, a hen with new chicks in the Tosa's garden, a storm gathering in San Diego Canyon, a sunset. At night we talked about innumerable things at the kitchen table, the innumerable things of our world and of our time. We laughed often together, and we saw eye to eye on the larger issues of our lives. The words we had were the right ones; we were easy and right with each other, as it happened, natural, full of love and trust. "Look," one of us would say to the other, "here is something new, something that we have not seen together." And we would simply take delight in it.

In the seasons and among the people of the valley I was content. My spirit was quiet there. The silence was old, immediate, and pervasive, and there was great good in it. The wind of the canyons drew it out; the voices of the village carried and were lost in it. Much was made of the silence; much of the summer and winter was made of it.

3

The first word gives origin to the second, the first and second to the third, the first, second, and third to the fourth, and so on. You cannot begin with the second word and tell the story, for the telling of the story is a cumulative process, a chain of becoming, at last of being.

Oh, it is summer in New Mexico, in the bright legend of my youth. I want you to see the very many deep colors of the distance. I want you to live, to be for an hour or a day more completely alive in me than you have ever been. There are moments in that time when I live so intensely in myself that I wonder how it is possible to keep from flying apart. I want you to feel that, too, the vibrant ecstasy of so much being—to know beyond any doubt that it is only the merest

154

happy accident that you can hold together at all in the exhilaration of such wonder. The wonder: I want to tell you of it; I want to speak and to write it all out for you.

I sometimes think of what it means that in their heyday—in 1830, say—the Kiowas owned more horses *per capita* than any other tribe on the Great Plains, that the Plains Indian culture, the last culture to evolve in North America, is also known as "the horse culture" and "the centaur culture," that the Kiowas tell the story of a horse that died of shame after its owner committed an act of cowardice, that I am a Kiowa, that therefore there is in me, as there is in the Tartars, an old, sacred notion of the horse. I believe that at some point in my racial life, this notion must needs be expressed in order that I may be true to my nature.

It happened so: I was thirteen years old, and my parents gave me a horse. It was a small nine-year-old gelding of that rare, soft color that is called strawberry roan. This my horse and I came to be, in the course of our life together, in good understanding, of one mind, a true story and history of that large landscape in which we made the one entity of whole motion, one and the same center of an intricate, pastoral composition, evanescent, ever changing. And to this my horse I gave the name Pecos.

On the back of my horse I had a different view of the world. I could see more of it, how it reached away beyond all the horizons I had ever seen; and yet it was more concentrated in its appearance, too, and more accessible to my mind, my imagination. My mind loomed upon the farthest edges of the earth, where I could feel the full force of the planet whirling into space. There was nothing of the air and light that was not pure exhilaration, and nothing of time and eternity. Oh, Pecos, *un poquito mas!* Oh, my hunting horse! Bear me away, bear me away!

155

It was appropriate that I should make a long journey. Accordingly I set out one early morning, traveling light. Such a journey must begin in the nick of time, on the spur of the moment, and one must say to himself at the outset: Let there be wonderful things along the way; let me hold to the way and be thoughtful in my going; let this journey be made in beauty and belief.

I sang in the sunshine and heard the birds call out on either side. Bits of down from the cottonwoods drifted across the air, and butterflies fluttered in the sage. I could feel my horse under me, rocking at my legs, the bobbing of the reins to my hand; I could feel the sun on my face and the stirring of a little wind at my hair. And through the hard hooves, the slender limbs, the supple shoulders, the fluent back of my horse I felt the earth under me. Everything was under me, buoying me up; I rode across the top of the world. My mind soared; time and again I saw the fleeting shadow of my mind moving about me as it went winding upon the sun.

When the song, which was a song of riding, was finished, I had Pecos pick up the pace. Far down on the road to San Ysidro I overtook my friend Pasqual Fragua. He was riding a rangy, stiff-legged black and white stallion, half wild, which horse he was breaking for the rancher Cass Goodner. The horse skittered and blew as I drew up beside him. Pecos began to prance, as he did always in the company of another horse. "Where are you going?" I asked in the Jemez language. And he replied, "I am going down the road." The stallion was hard to manage, and Pasqual had to keep his mind upon it; I saw that I had taken him by surprise. "You know," he said after a moment, "when you rode up just now I did not know who you were." We rode on for a time in silence, and our horses got used to each other, but still they wanted their heads. The longer I looked at the stallion the more I admired it, and I suppose that Pasqual knew this, for he began to say good things about it: that it was a thing of good blood, that it was very strong and fast, that it felt very good to ride it.

The thing was this: that the stallion was half wild, and I came to wonder about the wild half of it; I wanted to know what its wildness was worth in the riding. "Let us trade horses for a while," I said, and, well, all right, he agreed. At first it was exciting to ride the stallion, for every once in a while it pitched and bucked and wanted to run. But it was heavy and raw-boned and full of resistance, and every step was a jolt that I could feel deep down in my bones. I saw soon enough that I had made a bad bargain, and I wanted my horse back, but I was ashamed to admit it. There came a time in the late afternoon, in the vast plain far south of San Ysidro, after thirty miles, perhaps, when I no longer knew whether it was I who was riding the stallion or the stallion who was riding me. "Well, let us go back now," said Pasqual at last. "No. I am going on; and I will have my horse back, please," I said, and he was surprised and sorry to hear it, and we said goodbye. "If you are going south or east," he said, "look out for the sun, and keep your face in the shadow of your hat. *Vaya con Dios.*" And I went on my way alone then, wiser and better mounted, and thereafter I held on to my horse. I saw no one for a long time, but I saw four falling stars and any number of jackrabbits, roadrunners, and coyotes, and once, across a distance, I saw a bear, small and black, lumbering in a ravine. The mountains drew close and withdrew and drew close again, and after several days I swung east.

Now and then I came upon settlements. For the most part they were dry, burnt places with Spanish names: Arroyo Seco, Las Piedras, Tres Casas. In one of these I found myself in a narrow street between high adobe walls. Just ahead, on my left, was a door in the wall. As I approached the door was flung open, and a small boy came running out, rolling a hoop. This happened so suddenly that Pecos shied very sharply, and I fell to the ground, jamming the thumb of my left hand. The little boy looked very worried and said that he was sorry to have caused such an accident. I waved the matter off, as if it were nothing; but as a matter of fact my hand hurt so much that tears welled up in my eyes. And the pain lasted for many days. I have

157

fallen many times from a horse, both before and after that, and a few times I fell from a running horse on dangerous ground, but that was the most painful of them all.

In another settlement there were some boys who were interested in racing. They had good horses, some of them, but their horses were not so good as mine, and I won easily. After that, I began to think of ways in which I might even the odds a little, might give some advantage to my competitors. Once or twice I gave them a head start, a reasonable head start of, say, five or ten yards to the hundred, but that was too simple, and I won anyway. Then it came to me that I might try this: we should all line up in the usual way, side by side, but my competitors should be mounted and I should not. When the signal was given I should then have to get up on my horse while the others were breaking away; I should have to mount my horse during the race. This idea appealed to me greatly, for it was both imaginative and difficult, not to mention dangerous; Pecos and I should have to work very closely together. The first few times we tried this I had little success, and over a course of a hundred yards I lost four races out of five. The principal problem was that Pecos simply could not hold still among the other horses. Even before they broke away he was hard to manage, and when they were set running nothing could hold him back, even for an instant. I could not get my foot in the stirrup, but I had to throw myself up across the saddle on my stomach, hold on as best I could, and twist myself into position, and all this while racing at full speed. I could ride well enough to accomplish this feat, but it was a very awkward and inefficient business. I had to find some way to use the whole energy of my horse, to get it all into the race. Thus far I had managed only to break his motion, to divert him from his purpose and mine. To correct this I took Pecos away and worked with him through the better part of a long afternoon on a broad reach of level ground beside an irrigation ditch. And it was hot, hard work. I began by teaching him to run straight away while I ran beside him a few steps, holding on to the

158

saddle horn, with no pressure on the reins. Then, when we had mastered this trick, we proceeded to the next one, which was this: I placed my weight on my arms, hanging from the saddle horn, threw my feet out in front of me, struck them to the ground, and sprang up against the saddle. This I did again and again, until Pecos came to expect it and did not flinch or lose his stride. I sprang a little higher each time. It was in all a slow process of trial and error, and after two or three hours both Pecos and I were covered with bruises and soaked through with perspiration. But we had much to show for our efforts, and at last the moment came when we must put the whole performance together. I had not yet leaped into the saddle, but I was quite confident that I could now do so; only I must be sure to get high enough. We began this dress rehearsal then from a standing position. At my signal Pecos lurched and was running at once, straight away and smoothly. And at the same time I sprinted forward two steps and gathered myself up, placing my weight precisely at my wrists, throwing my feet out and together, perfectly. I brought my feet down sharply to the ground and sprang up hard, as hard as I could, bringing my legs astraddle of my horse—and everything was just right, except that I sprang too high. I vaulted all the way over my horse, clearing the saddle by a considerable margin, and came down into the irrigation ditch. It was a good trick, but it was not the one I had in mind, and I wonder what Pecos thought of it after all. Anyway, after a while I could mount my horse in this way and so well that there was no challenge in it, and I went on winning race after race.

I went on, farther and farther into the wide world. Many things happened. And in all this I knew one thing: I knew where the journey was begun, that it was itself a learning of the beginning, that the beginning was infinitely worth the learning. The journey was well undertaken, and somewhere in it I sold my horse to an old Spanish man of Vallecitos. I do not know how long Pecos lived. I had used

159

him hard and well, and it may be that in his last days an image of me like thought shimmered in his brain.

4

At Jemez I came to the end of my childhood. There were no schools within easy reach. I had to go nearly thirty miles to school at Bernalillo, and one year I lived away in Albuquerque. My mother and father wanted me to have the benefit of a sound preparation for college, and so we read through many high school catalogues. After long deliberation we decided that I should spend my last year of high school at a military academy in Virginia.

The day before I was to leave I went walking across the river to the red mesa, where many times before I had gone to be alone with my thoughts. And I had climbed several times to the top of the mesa and looked among the old ruins there for pottery. This time I chose to climb the north end, perhaps because I had not gone that way before and wanted to see what it was. It was a difficult climb, and when I got to the top I was spent. I lingered among the ruins for more than an hour, I judge, waiting for my strength to return. From there I could see the whole valley below, the fields, the river, and the village. It was all very beautiful, and the sight of it filled me with longing.

I looked for an easier way to come down, and at length I found a broad, smooth runway of rock, a shallow groove winding out like a stream. It appeared to be safe enough, and I started to follow it. There were steps along the way, a stairway, in effect. But the steps became deeper and deeper, and at last I had to drop down the length of my body and more. Still it seemed convenient to follow in the groove of rock. I was more than halfway down when I came upon a deep, funnel-shaped formation in my path. And there I had to make a decision. The slope on either side was extremely steep and forbidding, and yet I thought that I could work my way down on either side. The formation at my feet was something else. It was perhaps ten or twelve feet deep, wide at the top and narrow at the bottom, where there appeared to be a level ledge. If I could get down through the funnel to the ledge, I should be all right; surely the rest of the way down was negotiable. But I realized that there could be no turning back. Once I was down in that rocky chute I could not get up again, for the round wall which nearly encircled the space there was too high and sheer. I elected to go down into it, to try for the ledge directly below. I eased myself down the smooth, nearly vertical wall on my back, pressing my arms and legs outward against the sides. After what seemed a long time I was trapped in the rock. The ledge was no longer there below me; it had been an optical illusion. Now, in this angle of vision, there was nothing but the ground, far, far below, and jagged boulders set there like teeth. I remember that my arms were scraped and bleeding, stretched out against the walls with all the pressure that I could exert. When once I looked down I saw that my legs, also spread out and pressed hard against the walls, were shaking violently. I was in an impossible situation: I could not move in any direction, save downward in a fall, and I could not stay beyond another minute where I was. I believed then that I would die there, and I saw with a terrible clarity the things of the valley below. They were not the less beautiful to me. It seemed to me that I grew suddenly very calm in view of that beloved world. And I remember nothing else of that moment. I passed out of my mind, and the next thing I knew I was sitting down on the ground, very cold in the shadows, and looking up at the rock where I had been within an eyelash of eternity. That was a strange thing in my life, and I think of it as the end of an age. I should never again see the world as I saw it on the other side of that moment, in the bright reflection of time lost. There are such reflections, and for some of them I have the names.

the old woman Ko-sahn. She was close to me on the way to Rainy Mountain.

EPILOGUE

I ENTERED INTO THE Staked Plains and turned north. At some point in my journey it became clear to me that I was moving against the grain of time.

I came to a great canyon in the plain and descended into it. It was a very beautiful place. There was clear water and high green grass. A great herd of buffalo was grazing there. I moved slowly among those innumerable animals, coming so close to some that I could touch them, and I did touch them, and the long, dusty hair of their hides was crinkled and coarse in my fingers. In among them they were so many that I could not see the ground beneath them; they seemed a great, thick meadow of dark grain, and their breathing was like the sound of a huge, close swarm of bees. Guadal-tseyu and I, we picked our way, going very slowly, and the buffalo parted before us—it was like the careful tearing of a seam, stitch by stitch—and otherwise they paid us no mind. We were a long time in their midst, it seemed, a long time passing through. And farther on there were tipis, some of

Private Pohd-lohk, L Troop, Seventh Cavalry, Fort Sill.

Guipagho the Elder, Lone Wolf. I see
Mammedaty in this man; I know this
man in my blood.

them partly dismantled, and little fires gone and going out, embers smoldering, and many things were strewn about, as if a people were breaking camp. But there were no people; the people had gone away. And for a long time after that I followed their tracks.

And one day the earth turned red and the plains began to roll, and Guadal-tseyu bore me into the Wichita Mountains. And in the night I saw again some falling stars, and the next day it rained at Rainy Mountain, and I came upon the cemetery there and stood for a time among the stones. I heard the wind running, and there were magpies huddled away in the shadows.

There were old people in the arbor, and they were all very glad to see me, and they called me by my Indian name. And to each one, face to face, weeping, I spoke his name: *Mammedaty, Aho, Pohd-lohk, Keahdinekeah, Kau-au-ointy.* I saw the old woman Ko-sahn, who was my grandmother's close friend, who told me many things. She seemed to know of everything that had happened to us, to the coming-out people, from the beginning. She was very old, and I loved the age in her; it was a thing hard to come by, great and noble in itself. I remained there for many days, I believe. Guadal-tseyu ran with my grandfather's horses in the north pasture. From the arbor, in the early mornings and late afternoons I saw him there, how the low sun shone upon the rare red color of his hide. In the evenings we told stories, the old people and I.

When it was time to go on I rode north and west a long way, across many rivers, across the Washita, across the Canadian and the North Canadian, across the Arkansas and the Smoky Hill and the Republican, across the Platte and the Niobrara. There was no end to the land, and the land was wild and beautiful, and always there was a wind like music on the land.

In the Black Hills I breathed deeply among the trees, looking down from a hundred summits upon the deep swing of the plains to the sky. And when suddenly and at last I beheld Tsoai, it was the color of iron and it loomed above the earth, the far crest roving upon eternity.

166

This strange thing, this Tsoai, I saw with my own eyes and with the eyes of my own mind, how in the night it stood away and away and grew up among the stars.

I bore westward across the Powder River and the Bighorn Mountains, and after many days I took leave of the plains. The way was rocky then and steep, and it seemed that my horse was bearing me up to the top of the world. All the rivers ran down from that place, and many times I saw eagles in the air under me. And then there were meadows full of wildflowers, and a mist roiled upon them, the slow, rolling spill of the mountain clouds. And in one of these, in a pool of low light, I touched the fallen tree, the hollow log there in the thin crust of the ice.

GLOSSARY

A'dalk'atoi K'ado	"Nez Percé Sun Dance," 1883. (Kiowa.)
Ah-kgoo-ahn	"Putting Medicine on Him," the name of one of Kau-au-ointy's husbands, probably my great-great-grandfather. (Kiowa.)
Aho	My grandmother's name. The meaning is not known. (Kiowa.)
Cohn'	"Grandfather" or "Grandson," a familiar term of endearment. (Kiowa.)
Da-pegya-de Sai	The winter of falling stars, 1833. (Kiowa.)
Dine bikeyeh	The Navajo reservation. (Navajo.)
Dine bizaad	The Navajo language. (Navajo.)
Dypaloh	A conventional formula for beginning a story. (Jemez.)
Guadal-tseyu	Little Red, or red pony. (Kiowa.)
Guipagho	"Lone Wolf," the name of my great-grandfather. (Kiowa.)

Gyet'aigua	A conventional greeting. (Kiowa.)
Huan-toa	"War Lance," my father's name. (Kiowa.)
Kaitsenko	"Real Dogs," the name of an old soldiers' society. (Kiowa.)
Kau-au-ointy	"The Cry of the Goose," the name of my great-great-grandmother. (Kiowa.)
Keahdinekeah	"Throwing It Down," the name of my great-grandmother. (Kiowa.)
Mammedaty	"Walking Above," my grandfather's name. (Kiowa.)
Man-ka-ih	"Sleeve," literally. This is also the name of the storm spirit. (Kiowa.)
Map'odal	"Split-nose," the Indian name of a white man with whom the Kiowas had dealings in the 1880's. (Kiowa.)
Naat'aanineez	"Tall Chief," the Indian name for the town of Shiprock, New Mexico. (Navajo.)
Na'nizhoozhi	"The Place of the Bridge," the Indian name for the town of Gallup, New Mexico. (Navajo.)
Nizhoni yei	"Beautiful!" (Navajo.)
Pohd-lohk	Old wolf. (Kiowa.)
Qtsedaba	A conventional formula for ending a story. (Jemez.)
Seidl-ku-toh	A sweat lodge. (Kiowa.)
Set-angya	"Sitting Bear," the name of a famous chief, the leader of the Kaitsenko Society. (Kiowa.)
Sotobalough	A bread commonly baked at Jemez, much in evidence on feast days. (Jemez.)
Ta'dalkop Sai	Smallpox winter, 1839. (Kiowa.)
Tal-yi-da-i	"Grandmother," used here to designate one of the so-called "Ten Grandmothers" (Tahl-yope), ten sacred medicine bundles. (Kiowa.)

Tsegi	"Place among the rocks," sacred ground. (Navajo.)
Tsoai	"Rock Tree," the Indian name for the Devil's Tower in Wyoming. (Kiowa.)
Tsoai-talee	"Rock-Tree Boy," my first Indian name. (Kiowa.)
Tsomah	"Yellow Hair," the name of one of Pohd-lohk's wives. Keahdinekeah's sister. (Kiowa.)
Tsotohah	"Red Bluff." My second Indian name. (Kiowa.)
Zei-dl-bei	"Bad." (Kiowa.)